Benjamin Senior
Breathless

Anomie

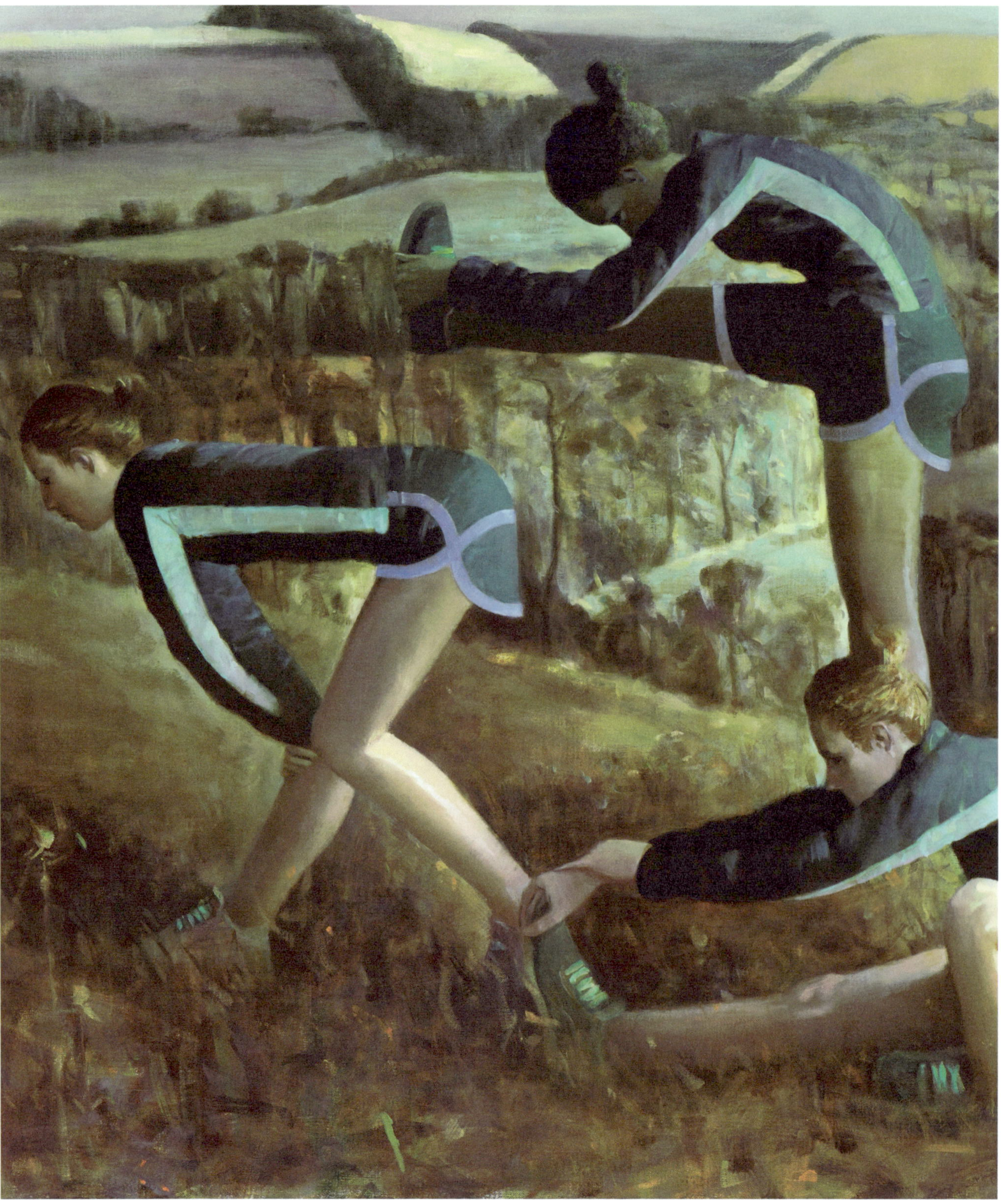

Sacha Craddock

Introduction

A woman lies flat on the ground beneath almond blossom, her legs pumping against a tree. Runners warm up, cool down, stretch their limbs and hug their knees. Moving in pursuit of further movement with lines running from ears to connect them to the reaffirming beat of another world, they appear impervious to cars and other people, unfazed by obstacles as they look to keep going. Black tracksuit tops with fluorescent stripes, orange bands, matching shorts and bare legs, stripped of identity, luggage, keys, money; even in twos or threes, they seem seriously, strangely, alone.

How do you convey a perpetual state of mannered movement with arms held high? The first view of a painting by Benjamin Senior betrayed an arch explosion of activity. What is this? Some form of revival of Chicago 1980s colour, patterning and graphic cartooning? Where does this madness, such a studied, opaque build-up of figure, reverberation, echoing and spiralling on tempera surface come from? But from Chicago, suddenly, later perhaps, to the early Renaissance where movement through space is echoed by a figure described once again, elsewhere, at the same time.

Senior is making work now, and has no need to reinvent the Renaissance experience of conveying movement. He has cartoons, comics, digital imagery and myriad other forms of visual language to consider in relation to paint – a whole gamut of heightened indulgence to enjoy, and yet his painting suggests a strong relationship with the art of the past. Senior's work might, for example, have something to do with Carlo Carrà, or to Italian futurism in general, or to late nineteenth-century impressionism and symbolism. It was useful to think, in situ, how gesture and movement in paintings at the Prado convey expression, and the other way around. Expression starts to lack exactly that when the subject is the perpetual state of everyday self-improvement in isolation. Sport may be expressive but fitness most definitely is not, yet a patterned prismatic feeling does build up. Senior's paintings of runners, swimmers, joggers, walkers and, more recently, people held close within in the street, morph from observation to a fixed state, a graphic surface quality.

Beacon Hill (detail), 2014, oil on linen, 100 × 150 cm

Nature is natural but the unnatural nature of painting takes the surface and finish elsewhere. We are looking on with a somewhat perverted observation, not feeling how it is from the inside. The patterns that are set up are both lovely and absurd. Clothed and naked, sacred and perhaps profane, serene yet almost comical, what the artist is saying isn't always entirely clear, the relation between him, us and the subjects still fascinating. He observes, we observe, but we are not being told. Limbs and loops and hoops settle into the surface, the grids and grilles of ironwork hold across, and language and fact are united in time. This quality of observation is also a touch voyeuristic: topless bathers seen through elaborate railings, girls exercising with rubber balls viewed from above, people standing or sitting on their own, their bodies the centre of our attention in various states of undress. Absurd, alone, in pairs, or a gang with no conversation, the body is the object for the walker, swimmer and runner as much as it is for us.

Senior's recent street scenes have demonstrated the evolution of his use of pattern, alluding to associative content, the heightened decoration of the street. The ornamentation and decorative architectural elements add another layer of pattern-based complexity. The figures emerge and disappear into the scenes to varying degrees, returning to the Prado, a scene with a wicker basket in a Joachim Patinir painting, or the head of a dog in a Goya oil sketch. A Balthus-like hiker posing in Senior's luxuriant painting of Beacon Hill, 2014, is independent and trapped. There is a struggle between the relation to the surface and the overall pictorial. The figures do not express but are attractive, their stylised depiction a shorthand for their conformity. From a compact rotation of action within the space, from trapped comic rendition, the sensibility and seriousness of painting fill the ground and a static still life makes the painting itself.

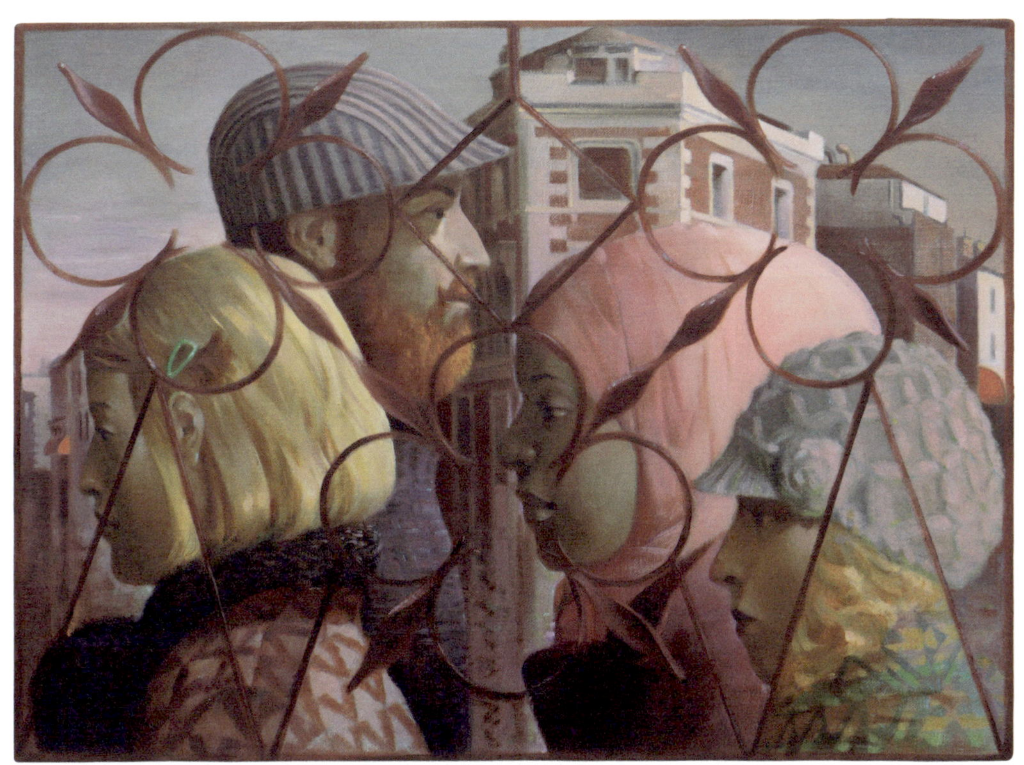

Palace Triangle, 2015, oil on linen, 61 × 82 cm

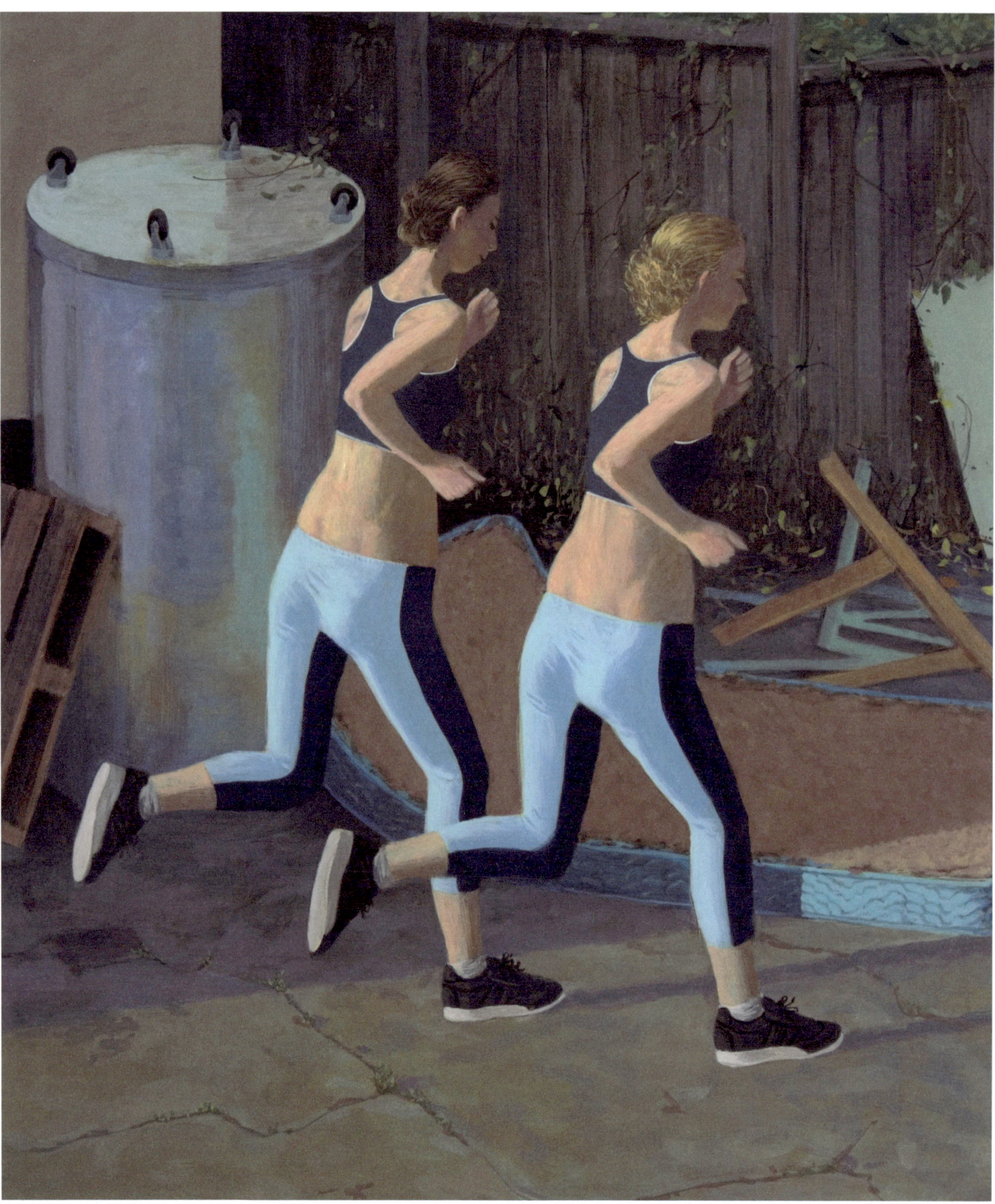

Ben Street

Benjamin Senior:
Choreographing the Moment

'... [the] pious English habit of regarding the world as a moral gymnasium
built expressly to strengthen your character in...'

George Bernard Shaw, *Man and Superman* (1903)

Figurative painting often invites a weighing of differences between its world and
ours. Benjamin Senior's images do this, but they go further, the disparity between
these two parallel realities somehow being played out within the paintings themselves. Figures stretch, dive, run, bend or stroll within settings that echo their
movements back to them. Patterns run across Speedos and into a tiled wall.
Piping on a sports vest gets picked up in the raked lines of a field. Senior's painted
subjects live in a world that is both animated and held in place by the movements
of athletic bodies. Every bent elbow or stretched back acts like the branch of a
diagram, charting the composition and keeping us always within each painting's
borders. As in the work of Nicolas Poussin – an artist Senior has been interested
in for some time – the painted world is a kind of corrected version of this one: more
elegant, more ordered, more anticipated. In both painters' works, the immediacy of
the lived world bumps into its corrected twin. In this encounter, Senior not only
creates unusual spatial and temporal dynamics, but captures some odd human
characteristics in the process too.

A disconnection between two worlds has characterised Senior's practice to date.
While studying painting at the Royal College of Art from 2008 to 2010, he found
himself immersed in formalist and neo-romantic discourses. While his peers often
explored the serendipitous moments of studio process, Senior's crisp and hard-
edged paintings kept the drama of the studio firmly in check. By using egg tempera,
Senior chose a medium that demands a method that is both contemplative and
sure: using tempera implies a slowness of hand, a calm and steady technique. That
his subject matter at this time centred on bodily exertion (inspired in no small part
by the proximity of the Royal College campus to the personal trainer hotspots of
Kensington and Battersea) suggests a further dislocation within this body of work

Two Runners, 2009, egg tempera on linen on board, 60 × 50 cm

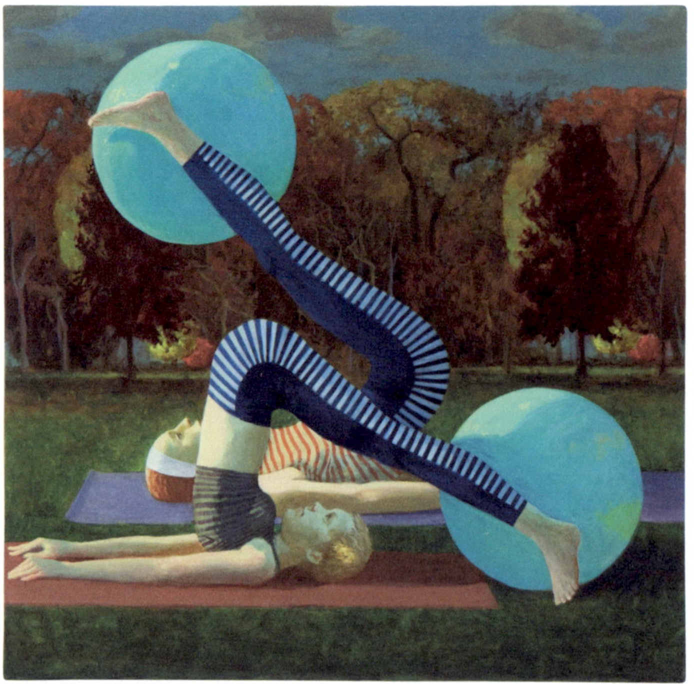

– the disparity between his subject and his method. Senior chose his subject matter by virtue of its distance from his own experience (not being an exercise fanatic himself), resulting in a self-imposed, singularly unromantic estrangement from the subjects he depicts.

It is this distancing, perhaps, that granted his early works the licence to embed surreal or uncanny elements within scenes of ostensible normality. A painting such as *Two Runners* (2009), which depicts two Lycra-clad female joggers on a city pavement blithely passing a pile of rubbish – namely an upturned wheelie bin and an old mattress – would invite a reading of social satire were it not for its startling departure from visual reality. The women's bodies are identical, and their doubling raises nagging questions that run through the artist's work as a whole: what levels of reality are we looking at here? What modes of representation are at work? To what extent is the visual language itself surreal? By not providing us with answers, Senior leaves us with an unsettling uncertainty as to his purpose or intended meaning: something is being articulated, clearly and eloquently, but quite what that is almost certainly remains unresolved in many viewers' minds.

The subject of physical exercise affords Senior's paintings scope to explore repetition, and, by extension, pattern. In *Tilt* (2010), first shown at his Royal College of Art

     Tilt, 2010, egg tempera on cotton on board, 60 × 60 cm

graduation show, two women practice yoga in a park, lying on their backs on coloured mats and swinging their legs right over their heads, each of them holding a large turquoise ball between their shins. Their two contrasting positions are like illustrations in a manual – figure one, figure two – and in being so imply a repetition that could go on forever. (Here, as is so often the case, Senior's figures show no signs either of exhaustion or of the *possibility* of ever being exhausted). The balls are located in opposite corners of the image, and beyond their iconographic meaning, become abstract forms in the work's formal conversations between colour, shape and line. The repetitions we might associate with exercise pulse through the painting like a drum: the repeated colour relationships in the screen of trees in the background, reds against yellows; the exercisers' striped leggings like undulating piano keyboards; even the women's faces in profile, stiffly vertical and self-assured. As a theme, exercise as the performance of visual pattern owes at least something to the theatrics of dance, and Senior has discussed the influence of Busby Berkeley's choreographed musical spectacles of the 1930s and Oskar Schlemmer's 'Triadic Ballet' of 1922. In both cases, the human body becomes abstracted to a pattern, the former through homogeneity and repetition, and the latter through bizarre, geometric modernist costume design. By isolating and repeating a single athletic movement, the human body becomes divorced from quotidian movement; divorced from itself. It becomes an abstraction.

For Senior, the culture of the interwar years provides exceptionally fertile ground. That a young painter should seek out works of art loosely assembled under the banner of 'the return to order' – the impetus among avant-garde European artists to revert to traditional subject matter and media after the horrors of the First World War – might suggest a conservative unwillingness to engage with his own moment. Yet for Senior, classicising works by Pablo Picasso, André Derain and Fernand Léger are component parts in a particular, sometimes marginalised history of modernism within which he positions his own practice. This modernist counter-current, much espoused by the American critic Jed Perl and articulated in writings by painter Jean Hélion, finds its roots not in Cézanne's fragmentary landscapes but in Corot's classicising ones, via Seurat's harmonic modernism, Derain's solemn later figuration, Balthus' clenched psychodramas, and Vuillard's transfixed domestic interiors.

In the years following Senior's graduation from the Royal College of Art, his work found an international audience with debut exhibitions at James Fuentes, New York (a two-person exhibition in 2011 with Ella Kruglyanskaya and subsequently a solo exhibition in February 2013); a solo exhibition at BolteLang, Zurich, in 2012; and a solo presentation at Monica de Cardenas, Milan, in September 2013. Audiences discovering Senior's work have drawn parallels with earlier precedents, such as US

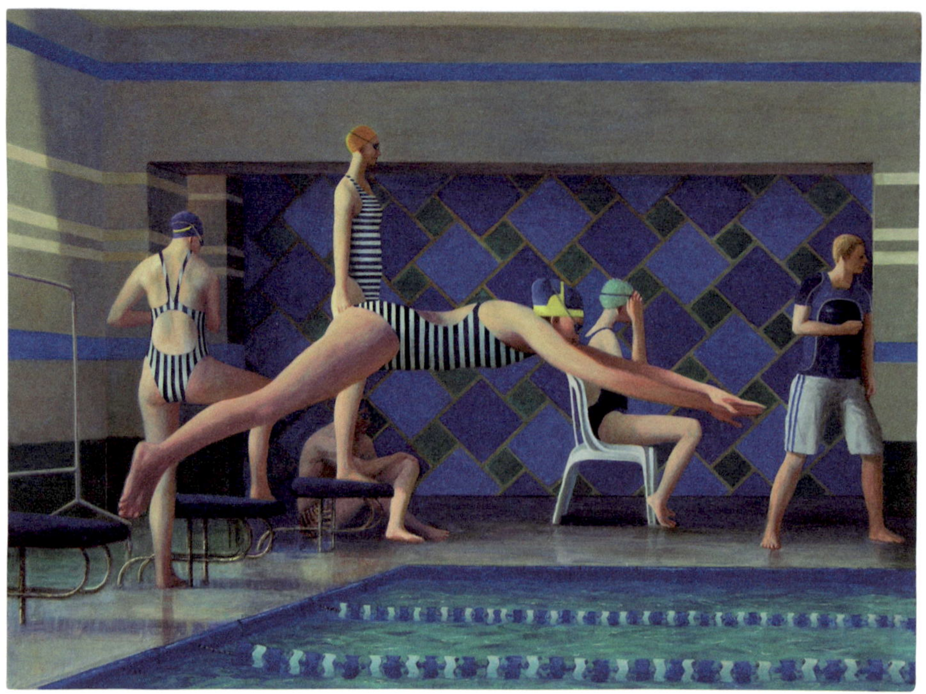

artist George Tooker's eerie social surrealism, the often revered Balthus or the Italian Novecento artists of the 1920s. Historically distant from the traumas that lent these painters their energy, Senior's work borrows their atmospheres in a spirit of revival. In this, he's not alone. One might usefully group his work with paintings by contemporaries who similarly return to somewhat neglected corners of early modernism, such as Kruglyanskaya, who brings together zippy fashion illustration with some of the complex awkwardness of Jean Hélion; Sanya Kantarovsky's listlessly elegant figures reminiscent of interwar cartooning; or Christoph Ruckhäberle's theatrical cubist dioramas. Each of these artists, like Senior, brings together a formal confidence and forcefulness with a wilful evasion of narrative clarity, in which figures, locked within the confines of elegantly delineated compositions, replay, seemingly endlessly, dramas of dissolution, detachment and disarray. For all of them, the dark and unloved corners of the modernist project provide material to articulate the confusions of the current historical moment: a call to disorder.

Following on from the yoga paintings, Senior's shift into new subject matter – swimmers (mostly female), depicted stretching and diving in sunlit, 1930s-style swimming pools – marked a step away from more evidently contemporaneous allusion. In a work such as *The Bathers* (2011), shown at Senior's New York debut at

The Bathers, 2011, egg tempera on cotton on board, 60 × 80 cm

James Fuentes gallery that same year, the modern world makes itself known only in glimpses: the familiar insignia of sportswear, maybe, or the straps of goggles tight against rubber caps. Such points of reference are subsumed to a greater whole in which the body locks into a grid-like structure at once reminiscent of Mondrian's Apollonian abstraction and the aforementioned Poussin's ruthlessly ordered compositional games. Notice that sequence of limbs, displayed on a loose curve that sweeps into the painting as a counterpoint to the room's blunt angles; it's a pattern borrowed from Poussin's rhythms of dappled legs in works such as *A Bacchanalian Revel Before a Term* (1632-3). And in Senior's tondo *Orphic Bathers* (2012), three figures in identical one-piece swimsuits stretch or prepare to dive at the lip of a pool; a Poussin-esque inverted triangle, generated by their stretching limbs, binds them together in perpetual deferral of bodily action. Senior's figures, like Poussin's, are employed as components within the painting's own scheme. A single unbent back, or a completed dive, and the painting's serenity can be broken in an instant. Order is something gently asserted here, for fear of being shattered.

p.35

In his solo presentation at South London's Studio Voltaire in October 2013, Senior created a suite of paintings that concluded his primary focus on the theme of exercise in his work, for now at least. In this exhibition, the theme of bathers met a gym ball-toting pilates class, and with it came a new approach to the human figure. In his tempera painting *Poolside Construction I* (2013) three swimmers in goggles and swimming caps are seen only from the neck up. Their heads overlap each other, creating a sequential spiral that moves in harmonious opposition to the curved railings that fill the painting's closest plane. The proximity of the viewer to the heads of the depicted swimmers does not bring with it the revelation of character that might be expected from such a close-cropped composition. Rather, as in the work of Alex Katz, closeness simply brings the painted surface into sharper relief. We bump against it, like a bee at a window. Painted depth, implied by the receding sizes of the subjects' heads, leads us only into looped pattern. The painting's world asserts itself as an inner one, its edges like borders shut against the outside. The heads, their eyes invisible under goggles, either don't, or won't, acknowledge the viewer's gaze. It's as if we, or they, are behind soundproofed glass.

p.36

In early 2014, Senior began to open up his painting to the urban environment, which acted as a sort of escape route from the exercise paintings. Focusing on the South London suburbs of Crystal Palace near which he was then living, his works from this time exhibit a markedly looser approach to mark making, something undoubtedly aided by his forays into oil painting. Where tempera allowed a kind of ready-made metaphor for the subject of concentration and mental focus in the swimming paintings – being synonymous with an almost meditative solitary practice not dissimilar to the loneliness of the long-distance swimmer – oil paint gave his works the chance to exhale a little, to unclench the jaw. In *The Grey Studio* (2014) – its title perhaps a nod to Matisse's red one, Senior's work having a more restrained, less hedonistic approach – a mostly nude model sitting on a chair arches her back, flexing her arms behind her head. Her full body is obscured by a pot plant, whose bushy components seem placed to both cover and act as equivalents for certain points in her body (head, breasts, bottom), in a curious *pas de deux* of human and natural forms. Seen from the artist's elevated position, the model is both less visible and, oddly, more so, since the plant's verticality emphasises her own; as in Senior's earlier works, the world is a diagram of the body, and vice versa. The furred tonality of the model's body, aided in no small part by Senior's novel use of oils, brings a sensuality to the painting that is all the more potent for being shown at arm's length.

In 2014 Senior made trips to his native Hampshire, painting and drawing *en plein air* with fellow painter Michele Tocca. This marked an important step away from the contained echo chambers of his swimming-pool paintings. Senior embraced the speed of hand and eye necessitated by making work outdoors, and the experience acted like a rush of air through his painting practice. Why Hampshire? In part for the childhood memories it inevitably embodied for the artist, which must infuse his work, Constable-style, with a wistful nostalgia for the past; and also, more curiously, according to the artist himself, because the fields there are 'so prim and tailored they look like sportswear'. Senior's drawing until that time had been characterised by two principal approaches: the expediently quick drawing made on public transport of details of a stranger's pose or outfit, to be stored for possible later use in a painting's composition; and the life drawing, done in the studio, of poses carefully orchestrated by the artist himself – those stretches, crouches and dives you see in the swimming and yoga paintings of previous years. In the works following the *plein air* excursions, though, the viewer has the sense of a corner being turned, into a more deeply symbiotic relationship both between painting and drawing as artistic practice (after all, that's what *plein air* painting, historically, has been about), and between man and nature as themes within the work. With a few notable exceptions, nature had been present in Senior's paintings in a (literally) contained form; cacti pepper the foreground of works such as *Ball Games IV* (2013), stretching and dipping in comic echo of the human figures alongside. In *The Stile* (2012), hikers rest beside a green fence, which cuts a horizontal swathe through the composition and acts as a grille through which (and by which) the landscape is seen and understood.

For his solo exhibition *Enclosure* at Grey Noise in Dubai in January 2015, Senior presented two distinct subjects, loosely divisible into urban and rural preoccupa-

p.82

p.60

p.98-99

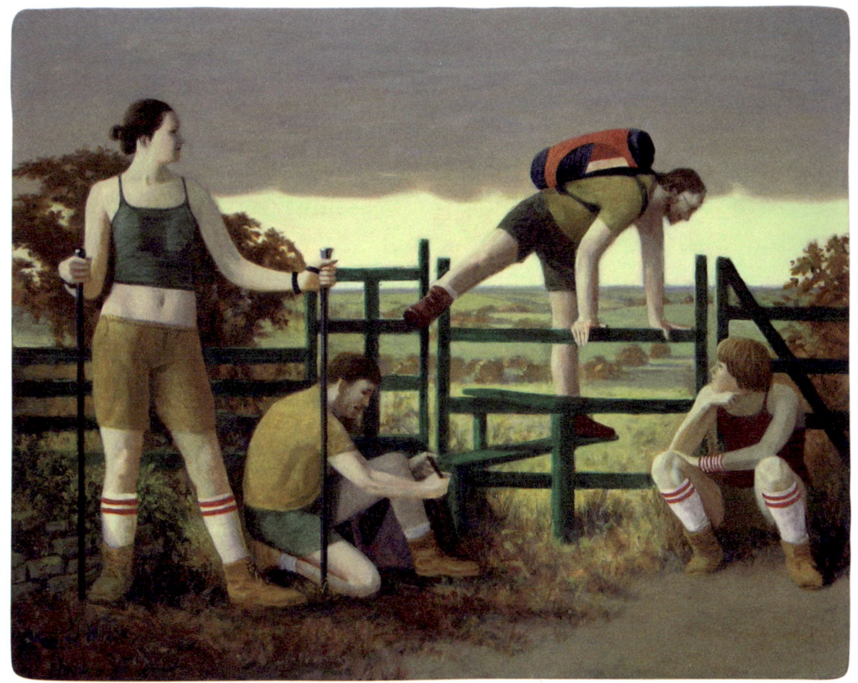

tions. In *Three Walkers on Beacon Hill (Spring)* (2014), the farmed landscape of p.79 Hampshire is spread out like a sequence of striped rugs (or, indeed, like the piping on the shorts and vests in the artist's earlier paintings). In the foreground, two figures, one standing, one sprawled on the ground, examine a map, to which one points with her walking poles; a third figure, his back to the viewer, shakes open a blanket in the middle distance. Although these three figures are contained within a right-angled triangle – a shape rhymed, if flipped, by the pointing poles – their arrangement within the landscape setting is one of correspondence, not contain-ment. And despite the painting's irresistible visual puns (that green striped T-shirt which, drawn deeper into the painting, becomes a furrowed field; the backpack's utilitarian design, picked up in the compartmentalised fields of the surrounding vista), the figures relax and spread within their setting. Senior's darting brush revels in the natural forms of nettles and long grass. In this work the viewer's proximity yields not the delicate artifice of a finely wrought surface, as in the earlier tempera work, but the physicality of paint *being itself*. For once, the romanticism he so long eschewed has found its way into Senior's work, however cautiously it appears.

Beacon Hill (2014) depicts three female athletes stretching, shown in profile and p.75 identically dressed in trainers, shorts and long-sleeved running shirts. Some of Senior's earlier gentle satire is at play here, as the distinctly urban attire of the

The Stile, 2012, egg tempera on cotton on aluminium, 40 × 50 cm athletes sits uncomfortably within the rolling landscape. Further, the discreet geometry of the figures' arrangements, picked up in the stripes of their clothing and their outstretched limbs (again, it's somewhat triangular) seems at odds with their immediate surroundings, which Senior paints with a looser hand than ever before. Despite this, the figures and the landscape rhyme with each other unexpectedly. The seated figure's stretched arm, grasping her toe, begins a gradual curve that continues as a low, tree-fringed hill. The line on the highest figure's striped arm carries on in the stripe of a hedge, far in the distance. Where visual rhymes generated a snappy surface tension in Senior's earlier work, here bodies seem to melt into the painted depth, lending the work's contemporary allusions – the shorts, the laces, the hairstyles – some of the gravitas of Renaissance painting. Consider the way Piero della Francesca makes the landscape anticipate the figures that inhabit it; similarly, in Senior's work, we cannot imagine plucking the figures from their setting, the landscape de-peopled. Each part makes the other, as you look. The interweaving of figure and ground, once held in almost geometric tension, is now warmer and softer. Colour sinks into the painting rather than sitting on its surface. In terms of Renaissance painting, we've gone from Florentine to Venetian.

p.63 In other recent paintings, by contrast, Senior seems to return to the deadpan Surrealism of his earlier work. In works such as *Rings IV (Autumn)* (2014), full-length figures pose behind decorative railings that fill the picture plane and hold the viewer somewhat at bay. A complex, gradually unspooling sequence of interlocking patterns – leggings, socks, flooring, railing – is picked out in egg tempera, its icy clarity of a piece with the work's sense of heightened reality. It has all the startling pin-sharp detail of a dream as experienced, rather than retold. The elegant dreamscapes of Surrealists like Paul Delvaux, or even René Magritte, are implied here, yet one might even go so far as to describe this branch of Senior's work as *magical realism*. It's that sharply delineated vagueness, the straight-faced telling of a fantastical tale. While everything within the image makes sense – no repeated figures, for example – the painting is nevertheless uncanny in its rightness, as so many of the artist's works are. The hula-hoops the two figures hold are foreshortened, egg-shaped. Your eye gets them tangled in the railings.

p.93 Four heads, sandwiched between iron railings and a decorative breeze-block wall, slide across the composition in Senior's painting *Commuters* (2014), a work representative of the artist's current preoccupations. We're in suburban South London, contemplating what we only ever glimpse: the patterns and shapes of other people's faces, hair and clothes. (Senior himself commutes into South London to get to his studio; the work's typically remote contemplation of other human subjects brings to mind, irresistibly, the image of the commuter who isn't *quite* a

16

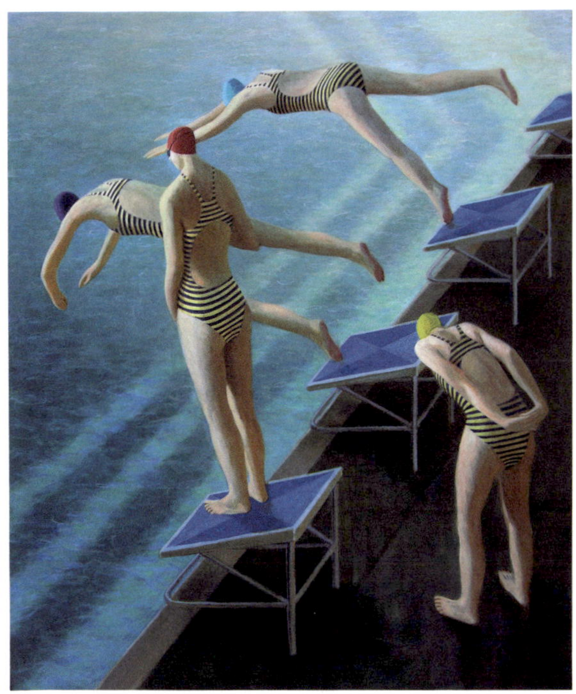

commuter). The railings reveal the figures' otherwise hidden geometries, using superimposed triangles (for the two women) to lock them into position, and quatre-foils and diamond shapes over the men's faces, which bind the evidently disparate protagonists into a rigid pattern like a flowchart. This rigidity invites us to supply the psychological and narrative layers that are absent from the literally buttoned-up characters within. The checks, stripes, spots and diamonds of the clothing act as harmonic components within a composition that makes Senior's jaunty visual patterns collide with all of the distanced and decidedly cool observation of a Seurat painting of Parisians sizing each other up in a public park. Every element of Senior's painting – nostrils, scarves, eyebrows, chins, shoulders, the seams on hats and coats – is a component of a discreetly complex ordering that, once seen, returns to itself, endlessly repeating, ticking like a pocket watch and breathing like a body in mid-dive in the moment just before it breaks the surface.

Shimmer, 2012, egg tempera on plywood, 60 × 50 cm

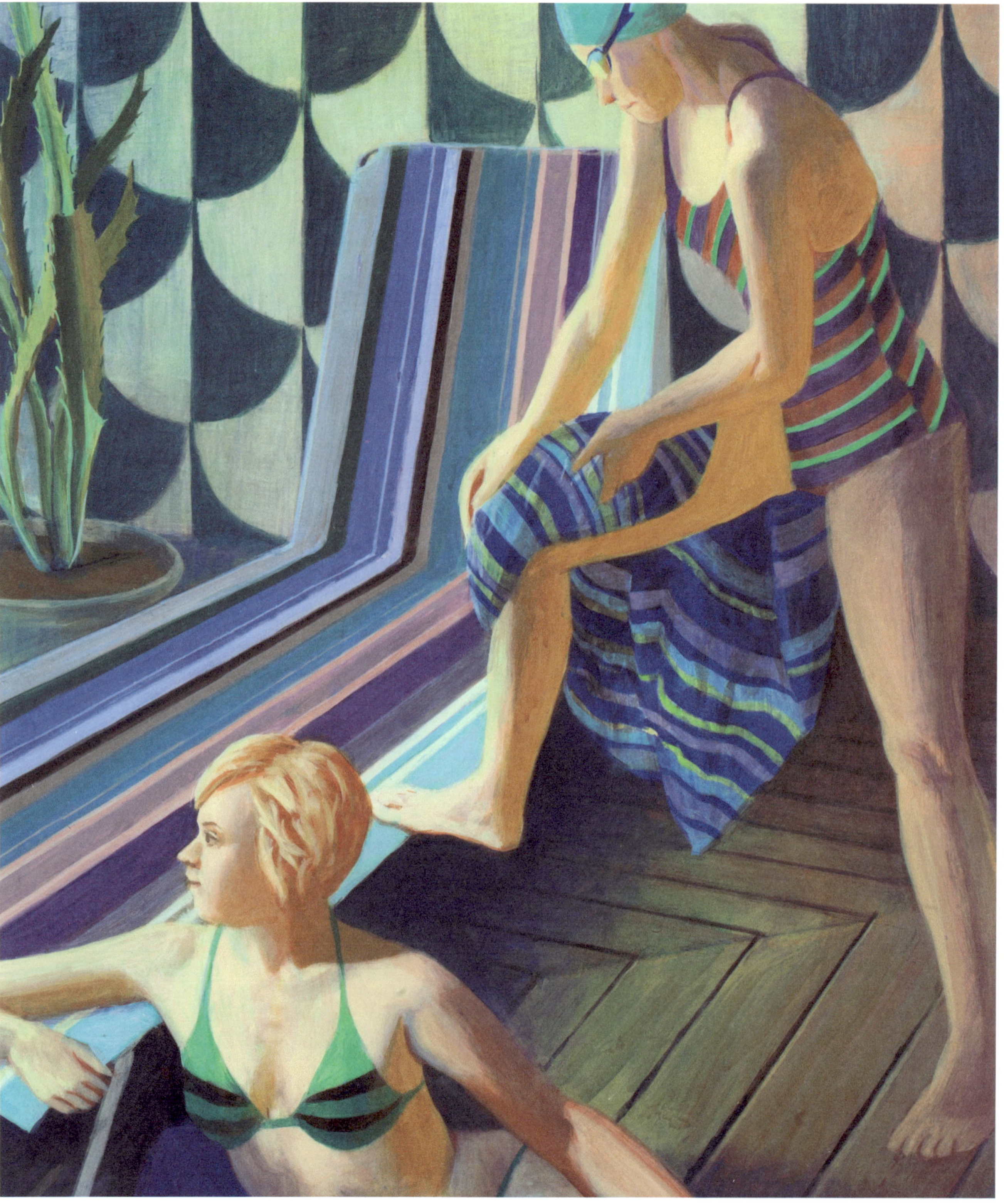

Gabor Gyory

Suspended Animation

Scene and Unseen

When viewing Benjamin Senior's paintings one is immediately struck by his impulse to richly describe the visible phenomena of his world. What is more, Senior depicts a world which at first feels very contemporary, familiar – knowable. Yet for all this familiarity, on closer inspection there is an unknowable covert logic beyond the world of empirics. Its creator makes himself known through geometric interventions that challenge the inherent rationality of his constructed world. In this way Senior's work sets up a dichotomy between the known and the mysterious. From intricately worked fabric to the rippling surface of a swimming pool rendered through the attentive work of the brush, the precise and generous furnishing of Senior's scenes serves only to make the void conspicuous.

Senior's world can be seen in relation to András Bálint Kovács' idea of 'Radical Continuity' and its opposite, 'Radical Discontinuity' developed by the Hungarian film critic in his survey of mid-twentieth-century European Art Cinema. The latter term applies to narratives that are fragmented as if invaded by the inconsistencies of the subject's psychological state. By contrast, Senior's world corresponds to Radical Continuity, in which 'the disconnected, alienated, or one-dimensional character of empirical surface reality'[1] is internalised. The consistent grammar of Senior's world hangs over the subject ominously, alienating and isolating the inhabitants of his paintings. The abundance of physical material that Senior depicts only serves to enhance the appearance of alienation in his subjects. Despite the abundant representation of the physical world, the resulting sense is that Senior's paintings are really, truly indicative of the fact that we can't know one another's internal lives.

Senior's scenes are marked by a sense of dislocation, highlighted by the various thresholds that run through his work. Each barrier presents a demarcation of different sets of elements, whether the physical environment, the personal space of the subjects, or their internal states. In his most recent works this separation has become more literally pronounced by the inclusion of a physical barrier between subject and audience: a painted ironwork grille. This barrier, which sits at the threshold of the picture plane and the scene behind, serves a variety of purposes for the viewer. The grille compels us to look through and in doing so transforms even the most casual of viewers into a voyeur. It is a provocation, on the artist's part, to the viewer's position.

The grilles, therefore, increase our sense of being alienated from the figures depicted, and of their isolation within the world they occupy. We are unable to know them, and we wonder what mysterious knowledge they themselves may hold. This is evocative of the *Samsara*, which in Buddhism represents the notion of ignorance of one's own state of existence, which in itself becomes a starting point for self-discovery. Seeing Senior's figures engaged in quiet and introverted but often disciplined activities suggests an aspiration for a form of self-knowledge, or self-actualisation. Despite their engagement in collective activity the figures in Senior's paintings seem alone, reminiscent of an ascetic monastic community in which the individuals have absolved themselves of personal attributes in favour of conformity to the ideals of their order. There is clearly a holistic relationship between the cult of exercise and spiritual fulfilment.

The habitual mode of the figures quietly and gently populating the scene seems to be a state of self-observation. There is an abundant and all-too-incumbent satisfaction that they have with their idleness which removes any sense that they may ever wish to leave their setting; and whilst the figures convey an almost inexhaustible solitude, in their transfixed poses they appear ultimately content to see the world pass unhindered, far too indifferent even to engage in a eulogy to inertia. Within the homogeneity of this world they seem particularly subdued, and lacking any voice of dissent.

This deficit of emotional or psychological depth in his subjects contrasts to the surplus of visual information in his materially rich spaces. The viewer's vantage point in relation to that of the subjects is privileged: it allows us to survey and absorb the entire surface of Senior's paintings and some of the many geometric and carefully composed intricacies of his rendered world. Whilst the subjects of the paintings appear so dedicated and singularly invested in their inward activities, they have no awareness of, or pay no attention to, the world they inhabit. Their introspection is almost vapid, and casts a shadow over the meticulously constructed scenes, rendering the appeal and complexity of their world seemingly incidental.

The figures show no sign of awareness of the viewer; there is no tacit acknowledgement of our presence. Yet the painting itself acknowledges the viewer's presence so

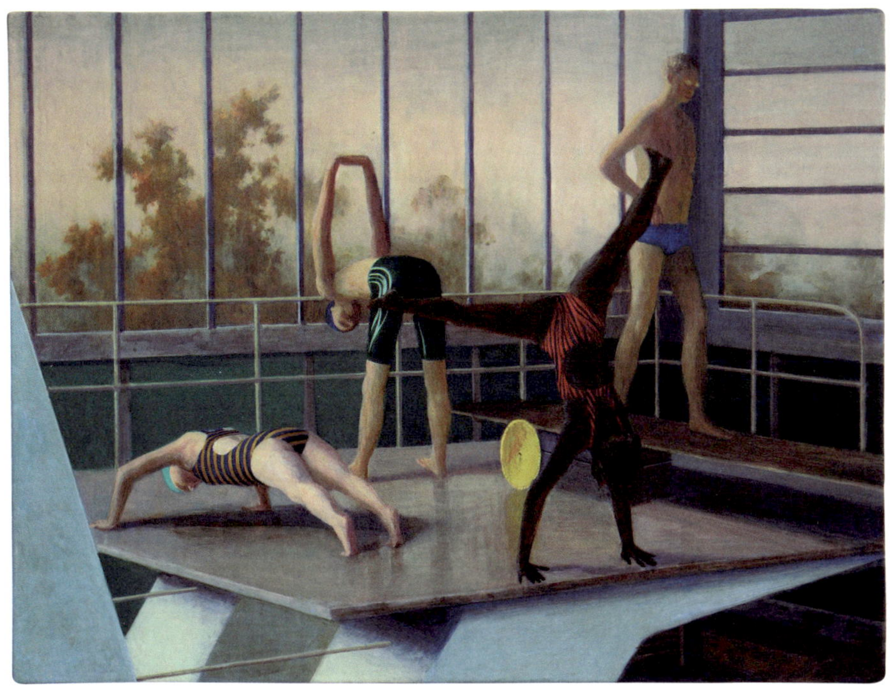

as to gaze back, to make the viewer observant of his or her own looking. The grilles, which hover between our world and that of the painted subject, perform a dissection of the scene beyond and serve to guide a way of looking. Yet this is not the casually sketched ironwork found in Manet's *The Balcony* of 1868, where the subjects are loosely restrained by the balcony's lightly gestural marks. For Senior the grille is a treacherous guide, often disturbing the illusory space of the picture, or like his recurring stripe motif, agitating the relationship between figure and ground. It is, therefore, an uneasy relationship between the observer and the observed.

Immersion and Retreat

Retreats typically occupy a liminal topography. Often located at the periphery of any political power they seek to excuse themselves from, and finding at this border a reassuringly comforting place to settle, the retreat holds a solipsistic position, the inhabitants often having fled or vacated communities of traditional power in search of assembled like minds at a more hospitable distance. Quite often they are located along coasts, like the rash of therapeutic communities such as Hadleigh Quay, which sprung up on Essex's nineteenth-century coastline, or in the manner of the community established on the cliff tops of Schleswig-Holstein overlooking the

Baltic Sea in Ernst Jünger's 1939 novel *On The Marble Cliffs*. The quality of Jünger's commune is firmly ascetic; weary of the impending recurrence of war between the major European Powers and their allies and dependencies, veterans of the First World War establish the commune at Germany's northernmost tip and devote themselves to the pursuit of cataloguing its flora and fauna. Senior's world possesses a semblance of these positions, just as ascetic and whilst not strictly in pursuit of generating a taxonomy of non-human species, they do inhabit a world which is highly ordered, as if they were the object of their own classification.

The figures within Senior's paintings have similarly sought refuge at the periphery, escaping the built environment to seek spiritual nourishment, often through the invigoration and renewal of engaging with nature, such as in 2014's *The Walker*. This work depicts the reassuring and familiar ease found in the English pastoral scene, where the figure can be both amongst and at peace with the rhythmic and soothing simplicity of the landscape. The hiking poles and backpack serve to harmonise the figure with her environment, the poles angled to become a pair of compasses, as if about to take the measure of nature.

For all the generous vantage points which the hilltop retreat suggests, the solipsistic attitude of its inhabitants proposes a greatly diminished view. Senior's painting *Three Walkers on Beacon Hill (Spring)* (2014) presents us with just such a viewpoint. Walkers repose on a hillside overlooking a sweeping panorama; however, they appear to look inward, perhaps because weary of looking out having been exposed to too much of an outer, shared and compromised world.

Parco dei Principei, a hotel designed by Italian architect Giò Ponti and built in 1967, occupies a similar topographical position to Jünger's inter-war commune in *On the Marble Cliffs*, but instead epitomises the relief and release of post-war Italy. High on a vantage point in Sorrento, its views overlooking the Bay of Naples are only disturbed by the decorative tiled surfaces in the ubiquitous and recurring hotel livery of white and pale and dark blue. Composed of similar geometric surfaces to Senior's paintings, the walls of the hotel jut confidently towards the sea.

The chic Mediterranean resort is suggestive of a process of erasure, indicative of a forgetting which enabled Italian society to move forward after the Second World War. For the hotel is located further around the Bay of Naples from the landing site at Salerno, where the Allies first gained a foothold on the European mainland at the beginning of their penetration into Nazi-occupied Europe. This is in contrast to Jünger's cliff-top community, which served as a site of memory for the horrors of the previous war, and equally as a process of denying what was to come. The

p.80

p.79

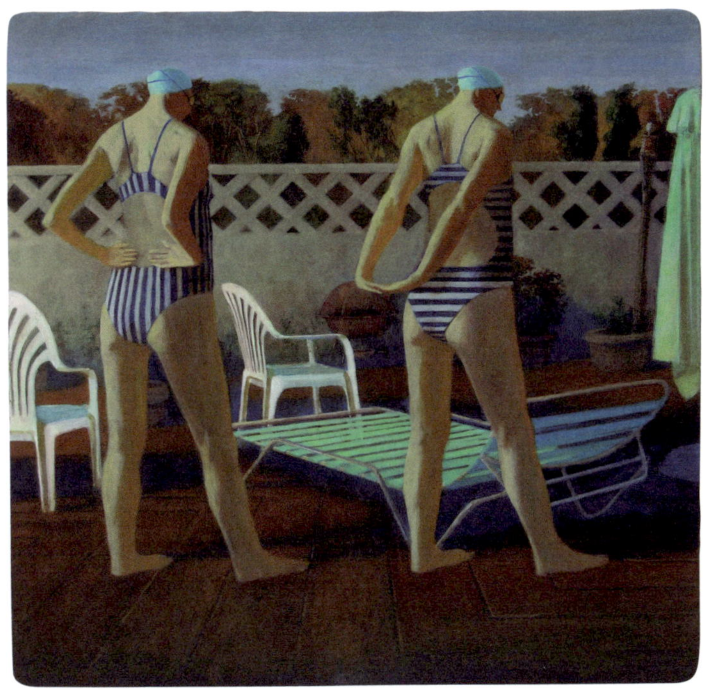

leisurely, resplendent idyll evokes an idleness, where experience is far from fleeting, where memory isn't briefly grasped, but endured, as the figures absorb the stasis of their unending state.

For Ponti's world, in post-Second World War Italy, and for the generation of other post-war Italian artists, architects and filmmakers, this spirited and superficial élan shaped a mask of denial. On the one hand it was a form of release at the close of long conflict, which like the hedonism of the twenties in Berlin, Zurich and London sought to obscure the dangers of memory and yet also to prove one's ability still to live, albeit with the brooding motivation of the experiences which brought it about. It also sought to establish through its past, prior to the conflict, a continuity which might enable the mode of social life once again to be restored.

The settings for many of Senior's narratives are the Modernist retreats of the spa or lido. For Senior these references are not incidental. In their insistence on a pervading culture of wellness, Senior's paintings imply an urgency to forget and to escape, characterised by his subjects' inward contemplation, and, mysteriously, a devotion to a narrative of immersive activity in which the paintings' viewers are not participants. These therapeutic locations in Senior's paintings are spaces for healing.

The Lido, 2012, egg tempera on cotton on aluminium, 45 × 45 cm

Motion and Stasis

Painting's motionless prerogative privileges the sense of stasis accentuated by the subjects' prolonged yoga poses. These transfixed positions embody a sort of discipline whose purpose is to suspend time. The dedication to suspending movement in aid of upholding the present serves as a singular, personal victory for the subjects. It is their attempt at withholding progress through suspending a whole world around their poses. The irony, of course, is that their very motion and energy are rendered inert in the process. All of the discipline, all of the associated carb-burn and toning is rendered powerless in a stasis that contravenes their aspirations towards progress, hampering their forward momentum. Rather it is the artist himself who is active and in control, determining his subjects' positions both in time and space.

Senior's cast is quite a specific demographic – there are no children in his world, no elderly people either. Their absence leaves his scenes populated entirely by the agile and healthy, the fit and fertile, people in their prime. The subjects demonstrate a dedication to bodily perfection which is indicative of a desire to suspend time by resisting the body's inevitable movement towards old age. The presence of crystalline, almost architectural cacti, which populate many of Senior's paintings, reflect the firm and ageless aspect of the supple bodies positioned between them. The flora of his scenes is the inverse of the weeds that sprout from the cracks in the decaying architecture of the paintings of the High Renaissance portraitist Giovanni Battista Moroni. These creeping patches of moss make comment about the mortality of the portrait's sitter, offering a sense of their increasing presence in a world in which they remain unchecked.

The tight but not encroached position of the figures within Senior's paintings is typical of a natural arrangement of distance found when figures assemble in social groupings. In psychology it is known as the *Zone of Attraction*, where people draw themselves together within a comfortable distance from one another, and the *Zone of Repulsion,* where they move apart to avoid an uncomfortable level of intimacy. The even and harmonious distribution of figures within the pictorial plane of Senior's work derives its logic from the location of the viewer's eye, from a point of alignment stemming from the source they choose not to acknowledge, which is ironic given the indifference they show to the world beyond their frame. The stances the figures adopt owe much to their context and setting, as well as constituting a language which is designed to be read. In Elias Canetti's work *Crowds and Power* he offers an interpretation of human poses, describing sitting or squatting as 'denoting an absence of needs, a turning in on oneself. The body is rounded and compact as

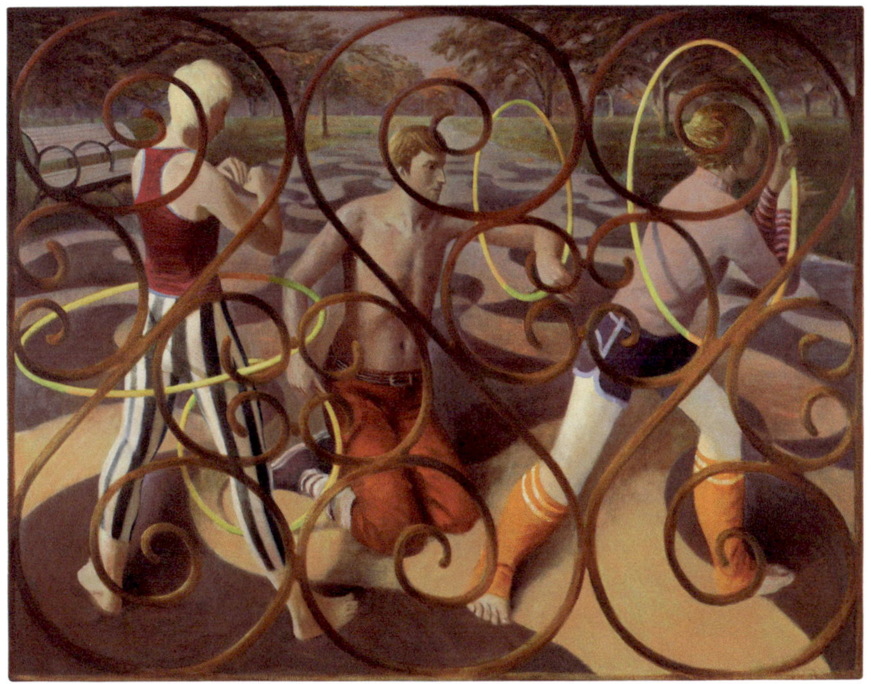

though expecting nothing from the world.'[2] For Senior, this language of postural sufficiency is sometimes mirrored by another figure within the image, as with *Green Interior* (2012). This synchronicity results in both figures becoming locked in an unspoken action, which preserves the interiority of their thoughts and the sense the figures are engaged in a community of practice.

The evident lack of spoken, verbal communication between the figures infers a sense that their postures possess a discernible meaning. Canetti notes that posture also possesses a grammar. 'People normally stand before they begin to walk or run, and because standing is thus the antecedent of all motion, a standing man creates an impression of energy which is as yet unused. Standing is the central position.'[3] This sense of grammar is also a painterly one. It is a harmony of colour, but also of the painter's sensibility in conceiving a world from a single vantage point.

Activity is sometimes centred around paraphernalia of fitness, such as the spring-board, hula hoop or gym ball. The presence of these items littered across the scene is reminiscent of the sort of enigmatic humanist, musical, geometric and scientific objects placed in Renaissance paintings. In Senior's world these innocuous props take on a significance for the members of his communities approaching that of li-turgical instruments or holy reliquaries. Held in a cantilevered stance, they do more

Rings VIII (Parade), 2014, oil on linen, 120 × 150 cm

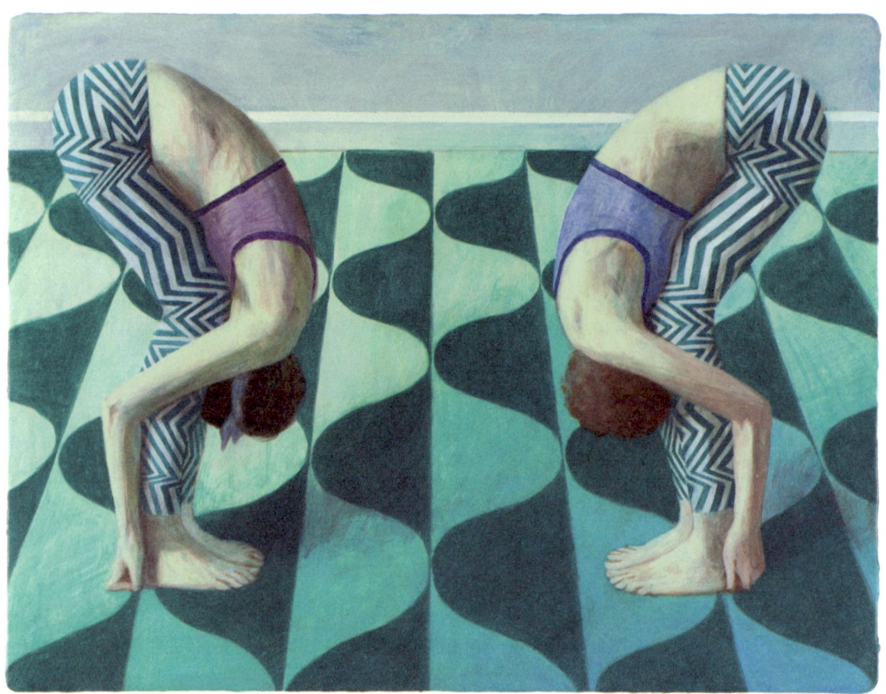

than provide balance. The geometric form of the object transforms the figure, assimilating it into the pattern of its environment. Here the body becomes a compositional element, synthesising the physical practice with the painterly – the immersive practice of balancing colours, the interweaving of the visual rhythms. When confronting Senior's work, are we viewing scenes of physical exercise or are we in fact witnessing the artist's own spiritual exercises?

1. Bálint Kovács, András, *Screening Modernism, European Art Cinema 1950-1980*, The University of Chicago Press, 2007, p.126
2. Canetti, Elias, *Crowds and Power*, The Continuum Press, New York, 1978, p.393
3. Ibid.

Green Interior, 2012, egg tempera on cotton on aluminium, 35 × 45 cm

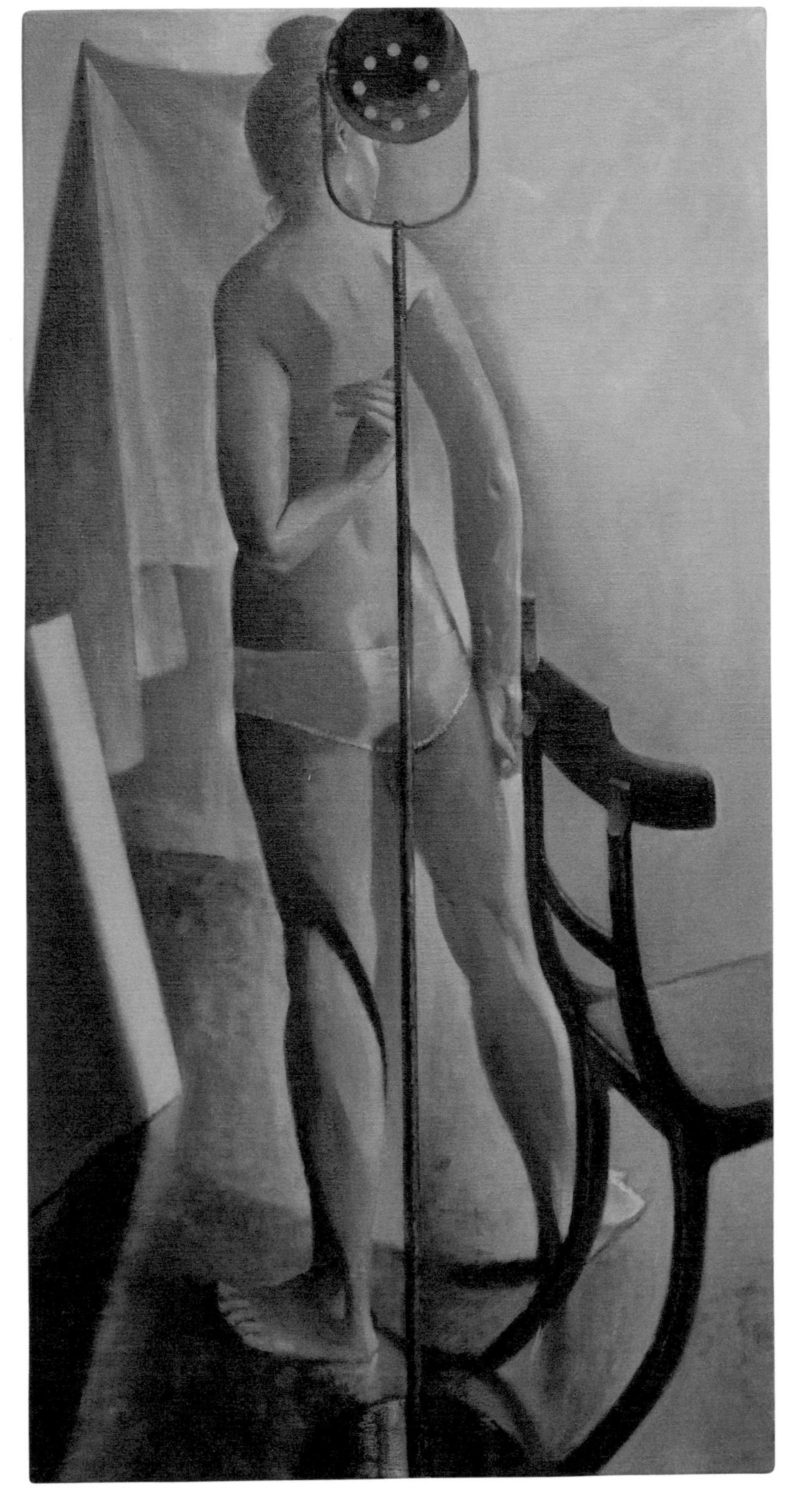

The Grey Studio II, 2014, oil on linen, 150 × 75 cm

Minaret, 2012
Egg tempera on cotton on aluminium, 45 × 30 cm

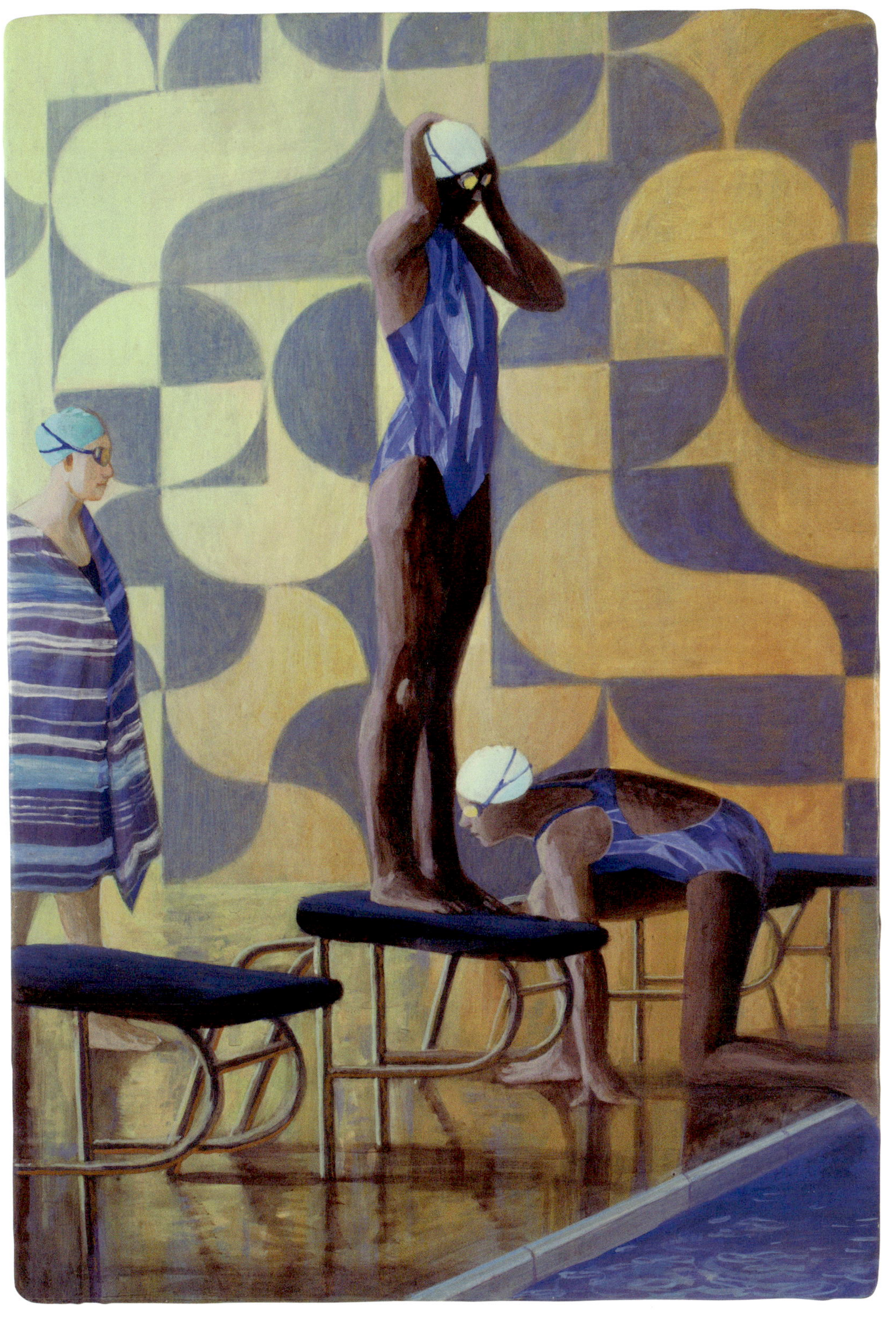

The Pool, 2013
Egg tempera on cotton on aluminium, 40 × 60 cm

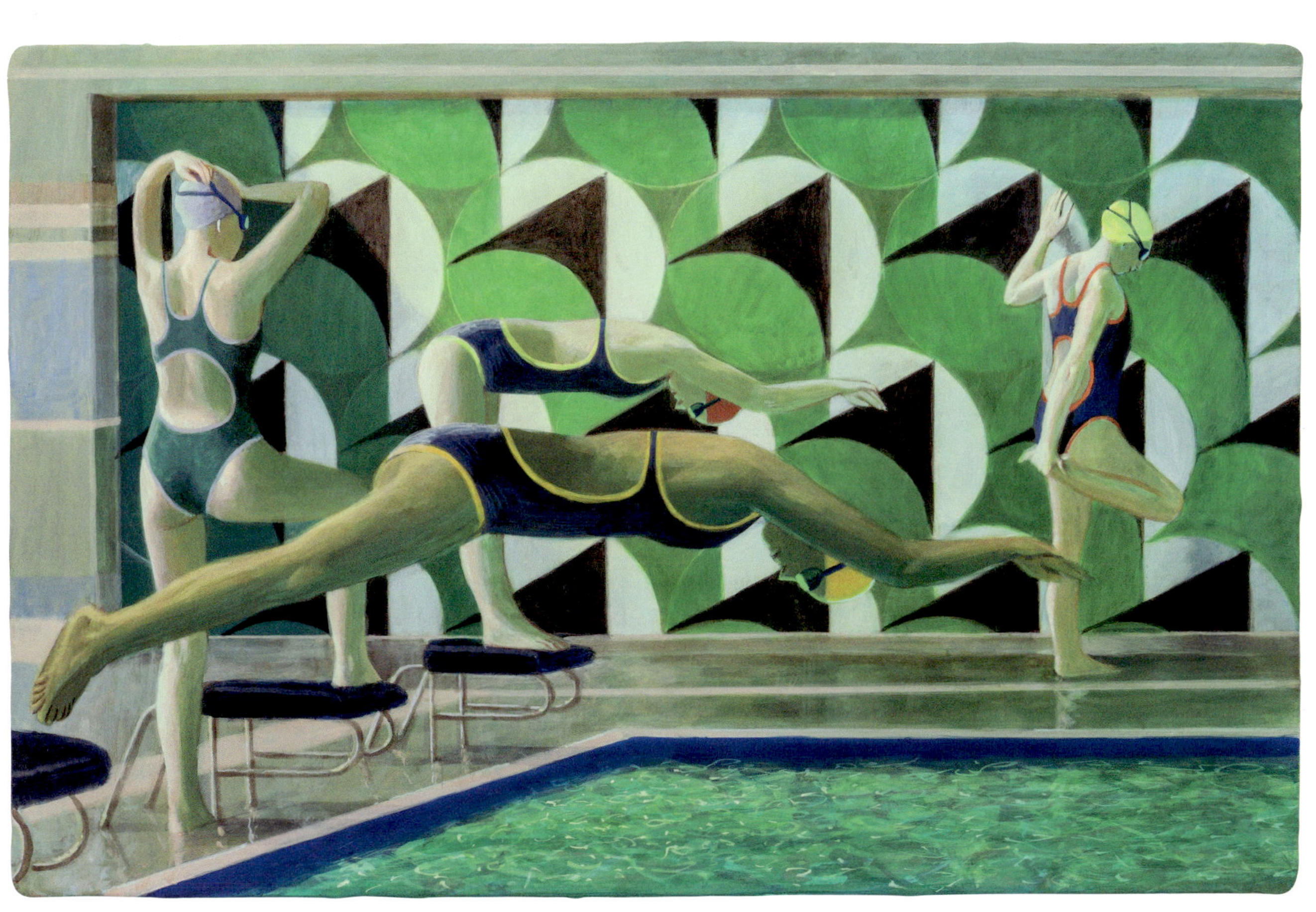

Forward Approach, 2011
Egg tempera on cotton on aluminium, 40 × 35 cm

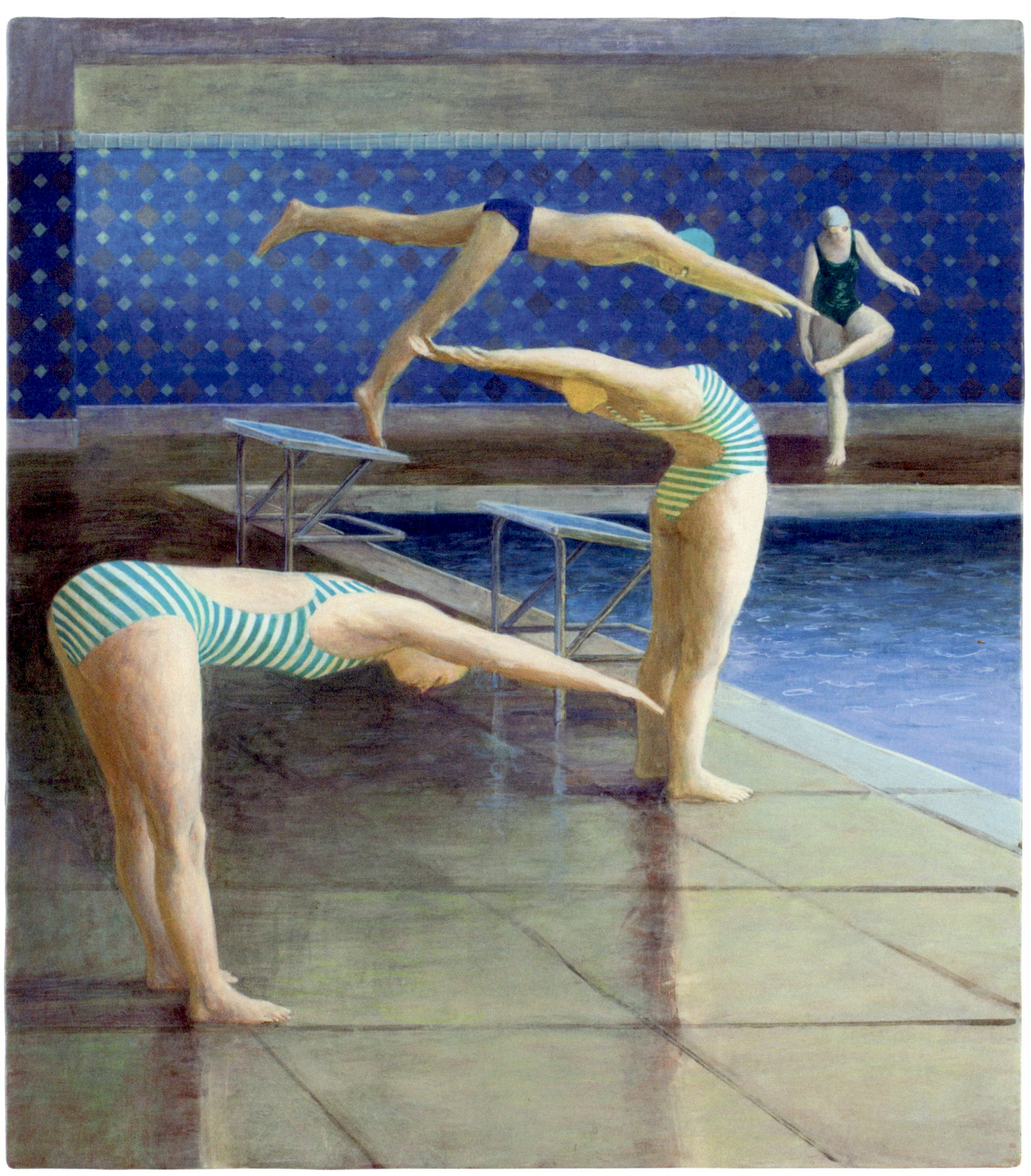

Orphic Bathers, 2012
Egg tempera on cotton on aluminium, ⌀50 cm

Following spread:

Poolside Construction I, 2013
Egg tempera on cotton on plywood, 50 × 40 cm

Poolside Construction II, 2013
Egg tempera on cotton on plywood, 50 × 40 cm

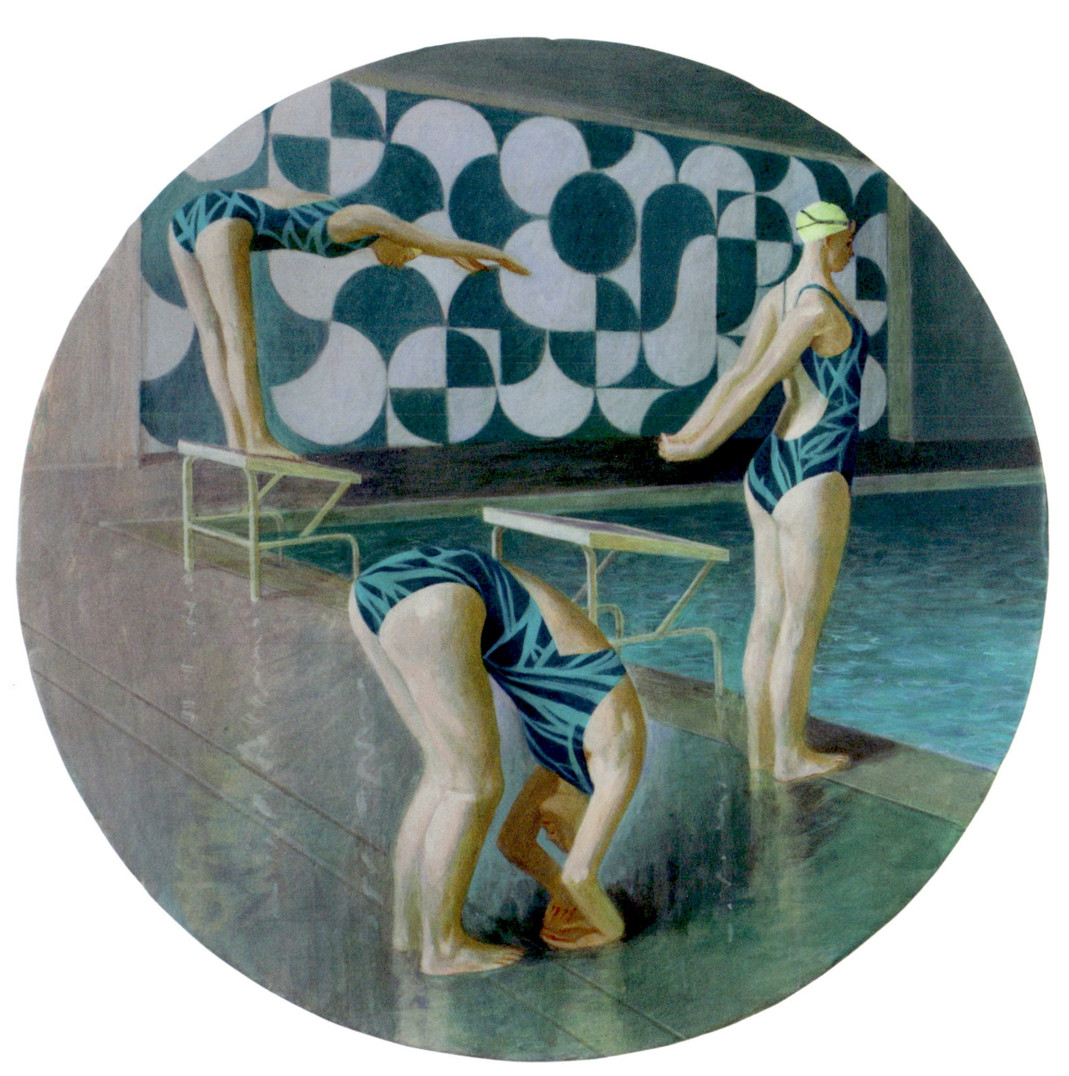

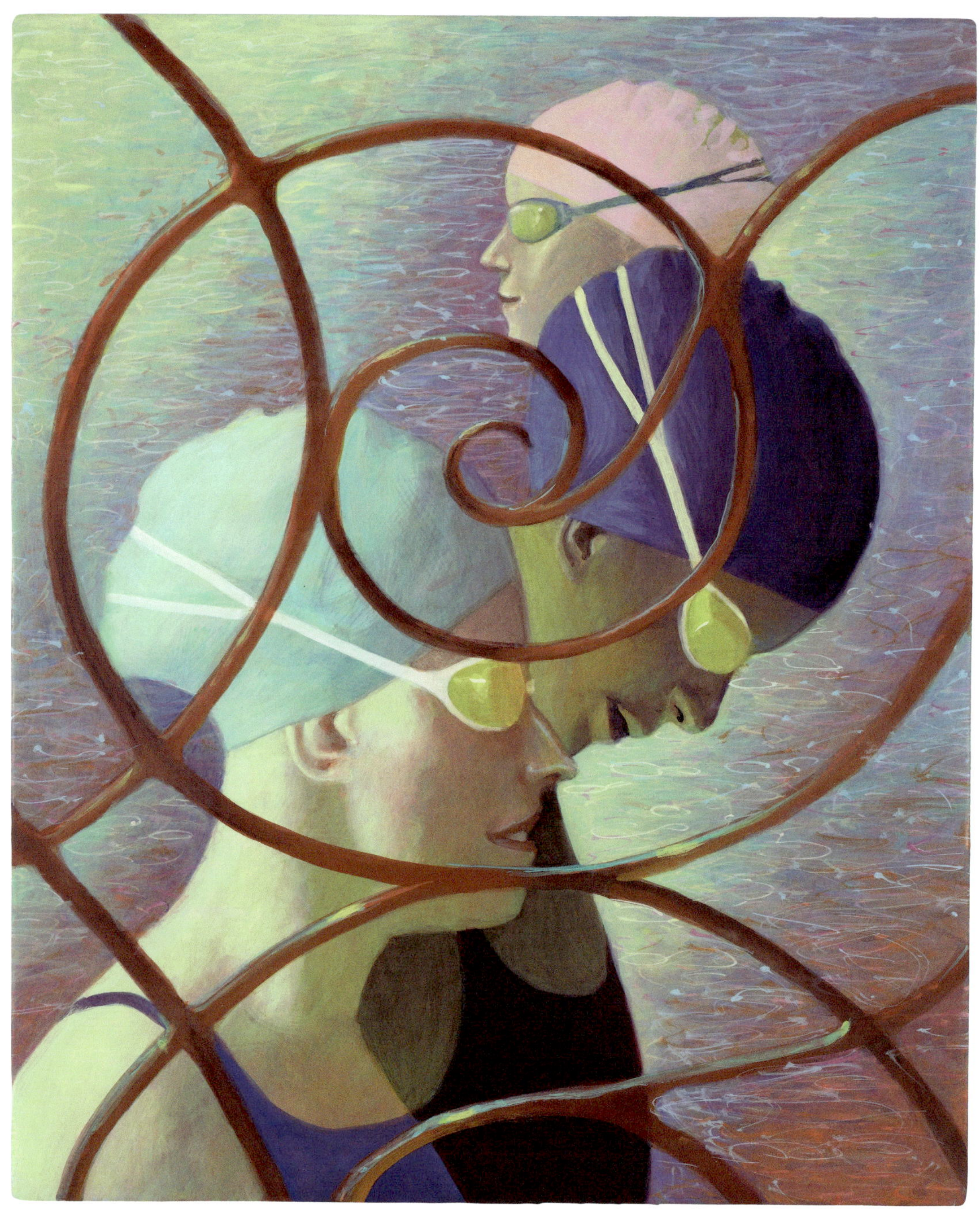

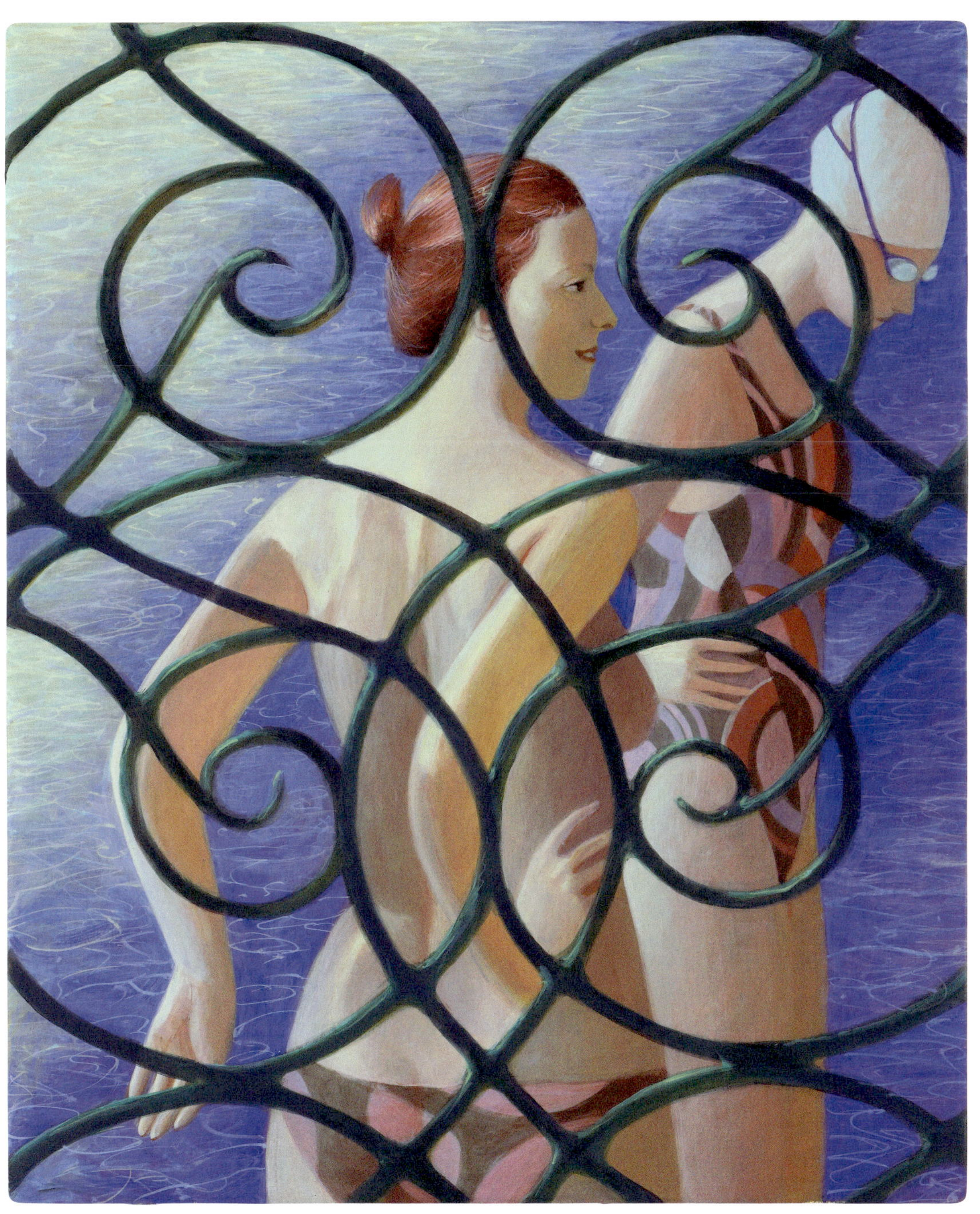

Poolside, 2012
Egg tempera on cotton on aluminium, 30 × 45 cm

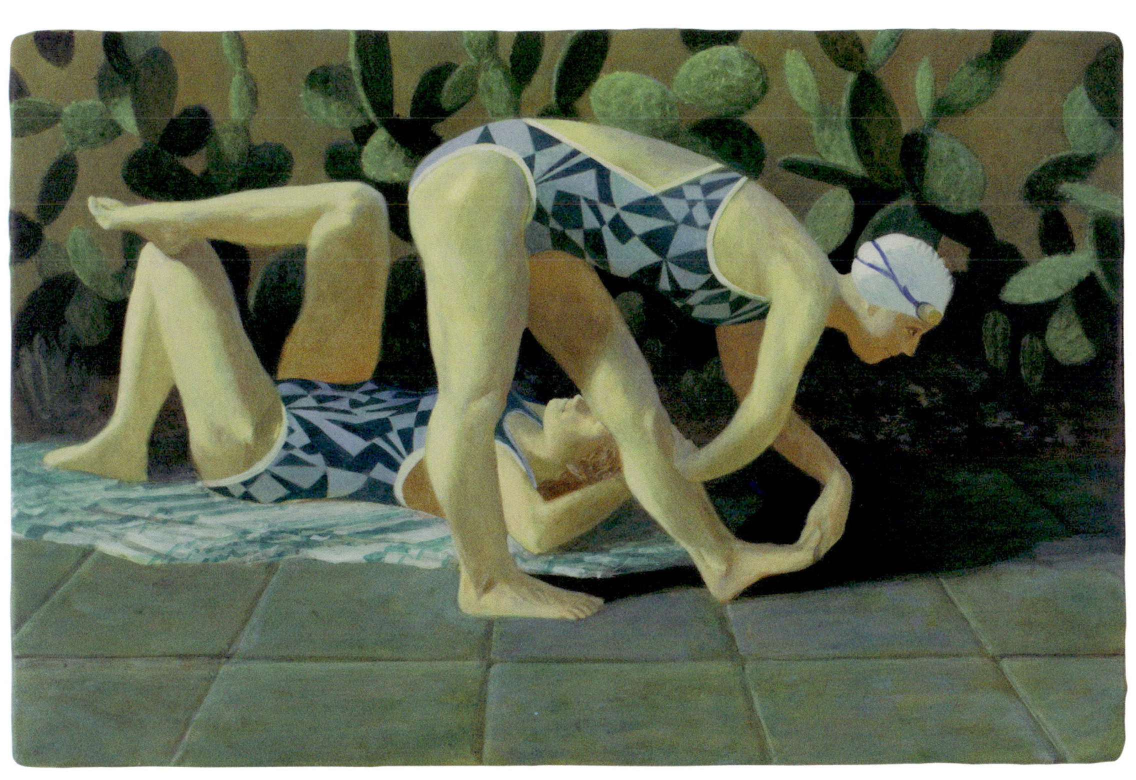

Two Bathers, 2012
Egg tempera on cotton on aluminium, 60 × 50 cm

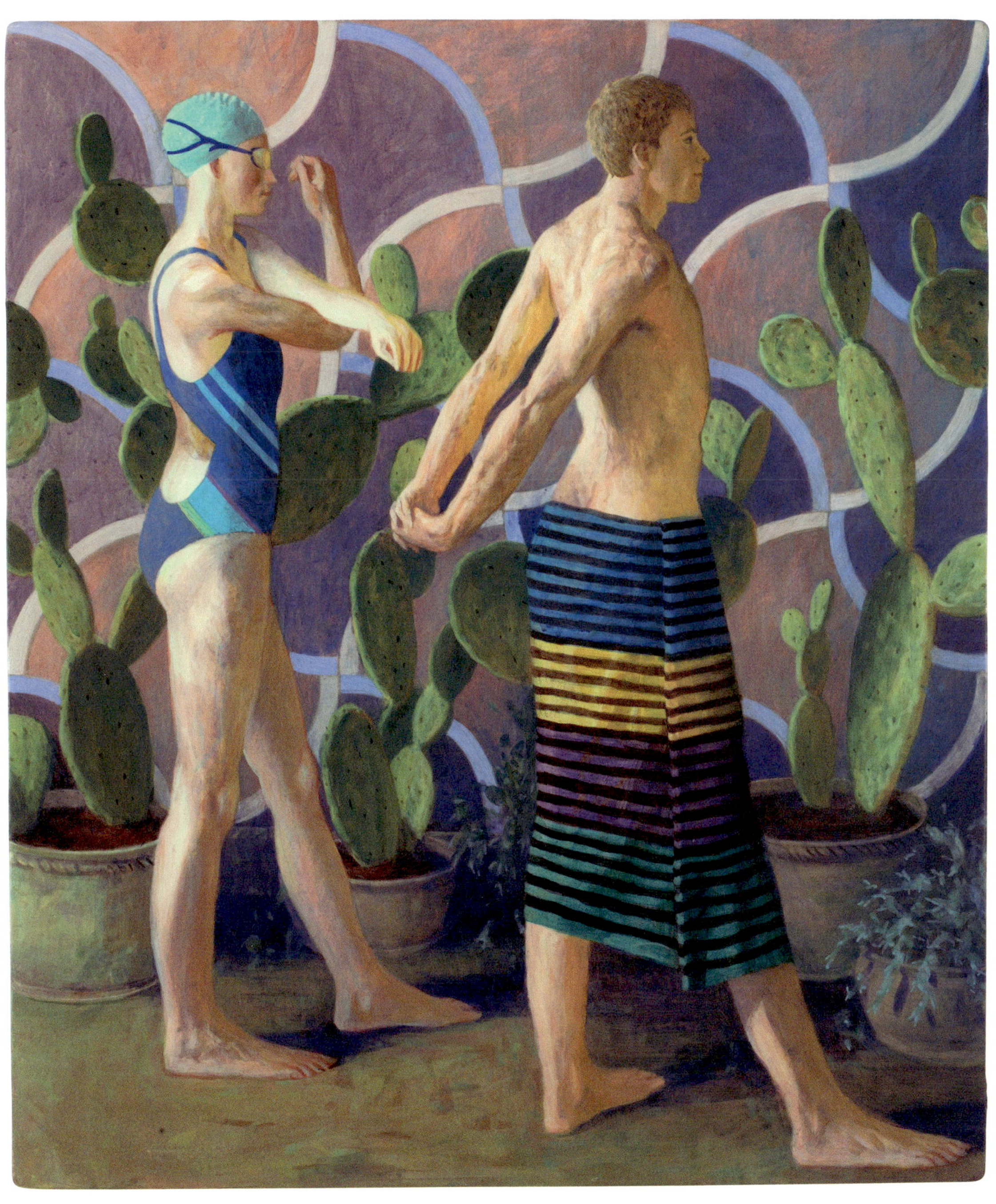

Sunbomb, 2012
Egg tempera on cotton on aluminium, 70 × 50 cm

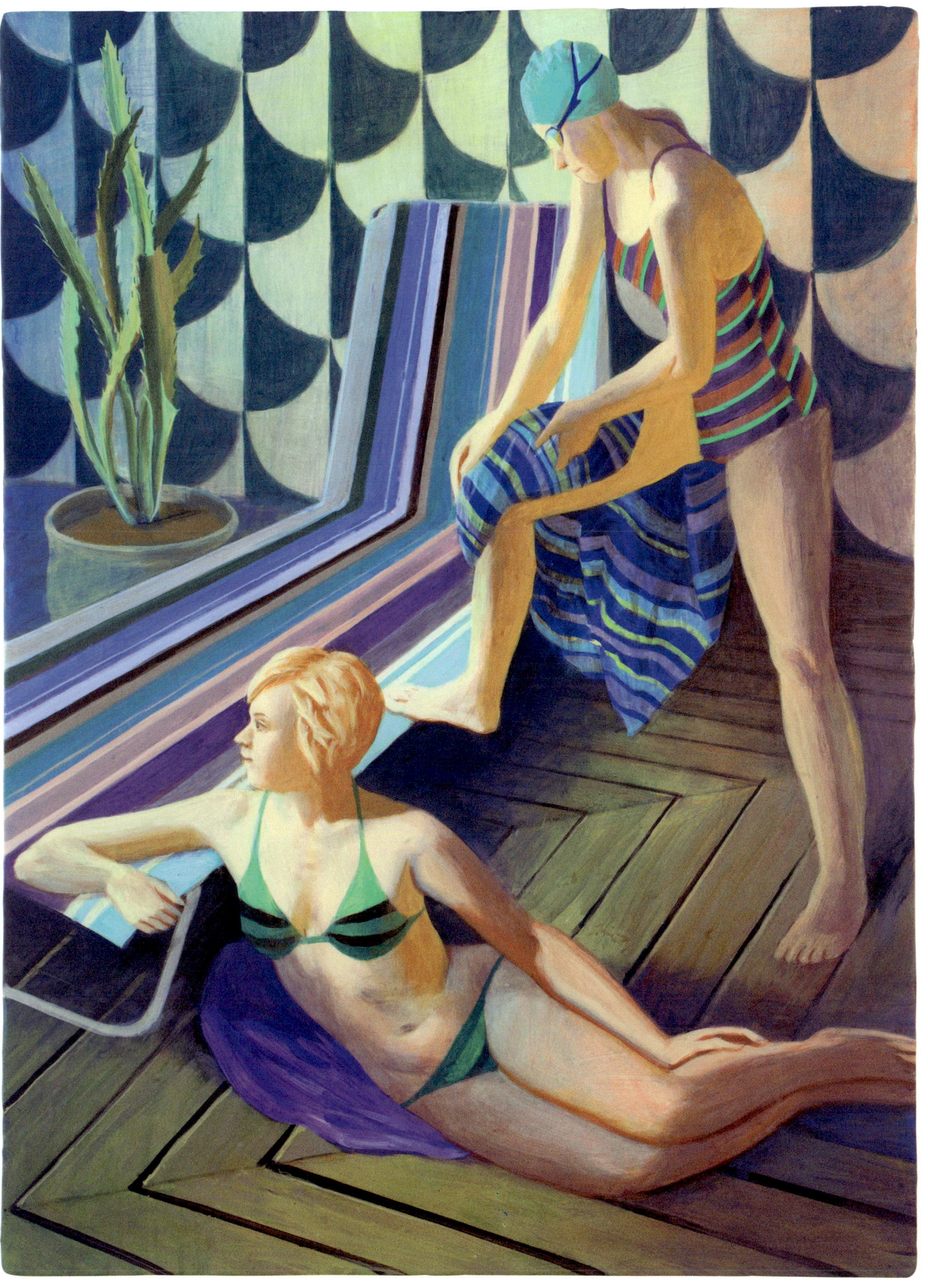

Sunbathers, 2013
Egg tempera on cotton on aluminium, 40 × 60 cm

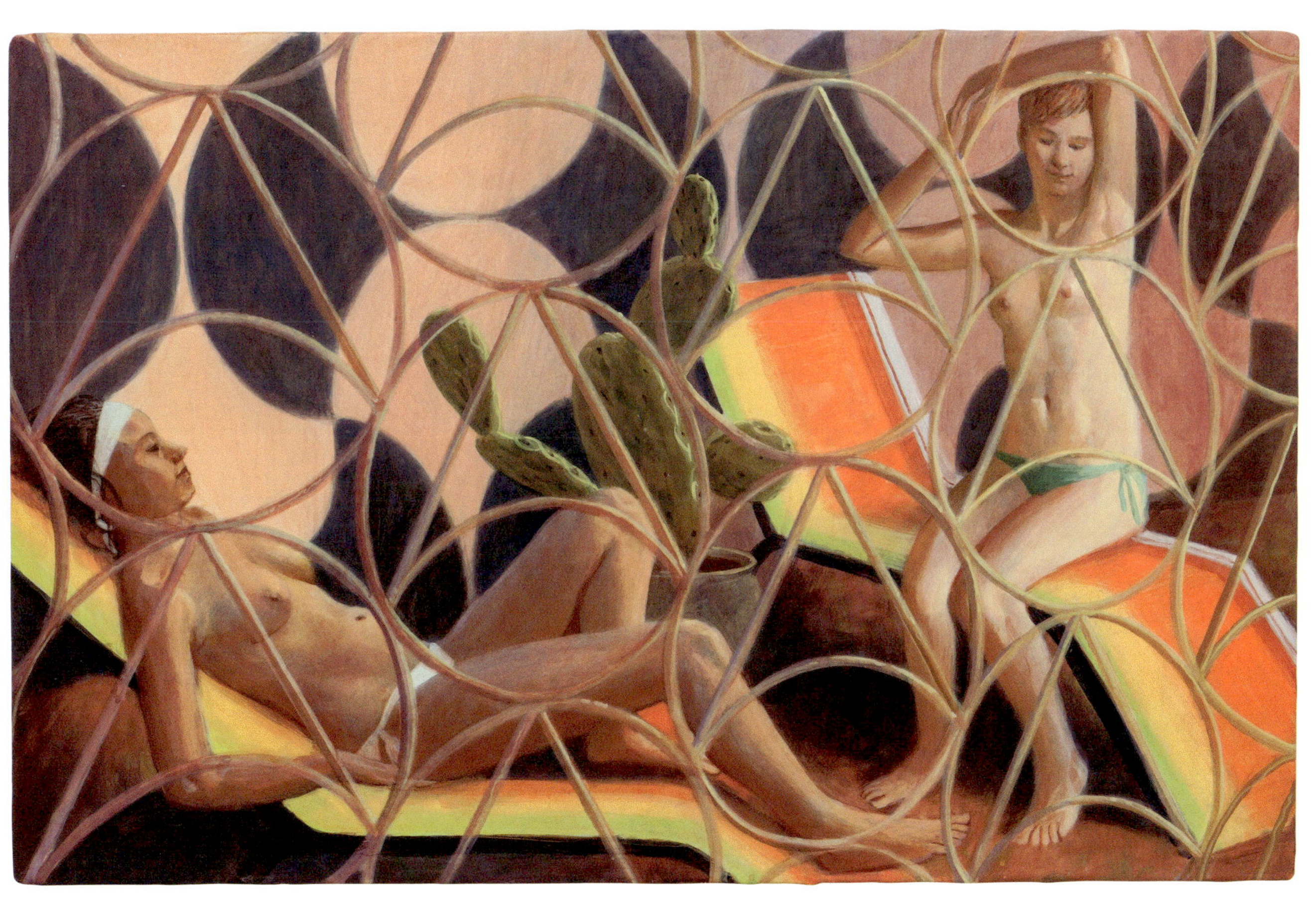

Fernand's Dream II, 2013
Egg tempera on cotton on aluminium, 60 × 60 cm

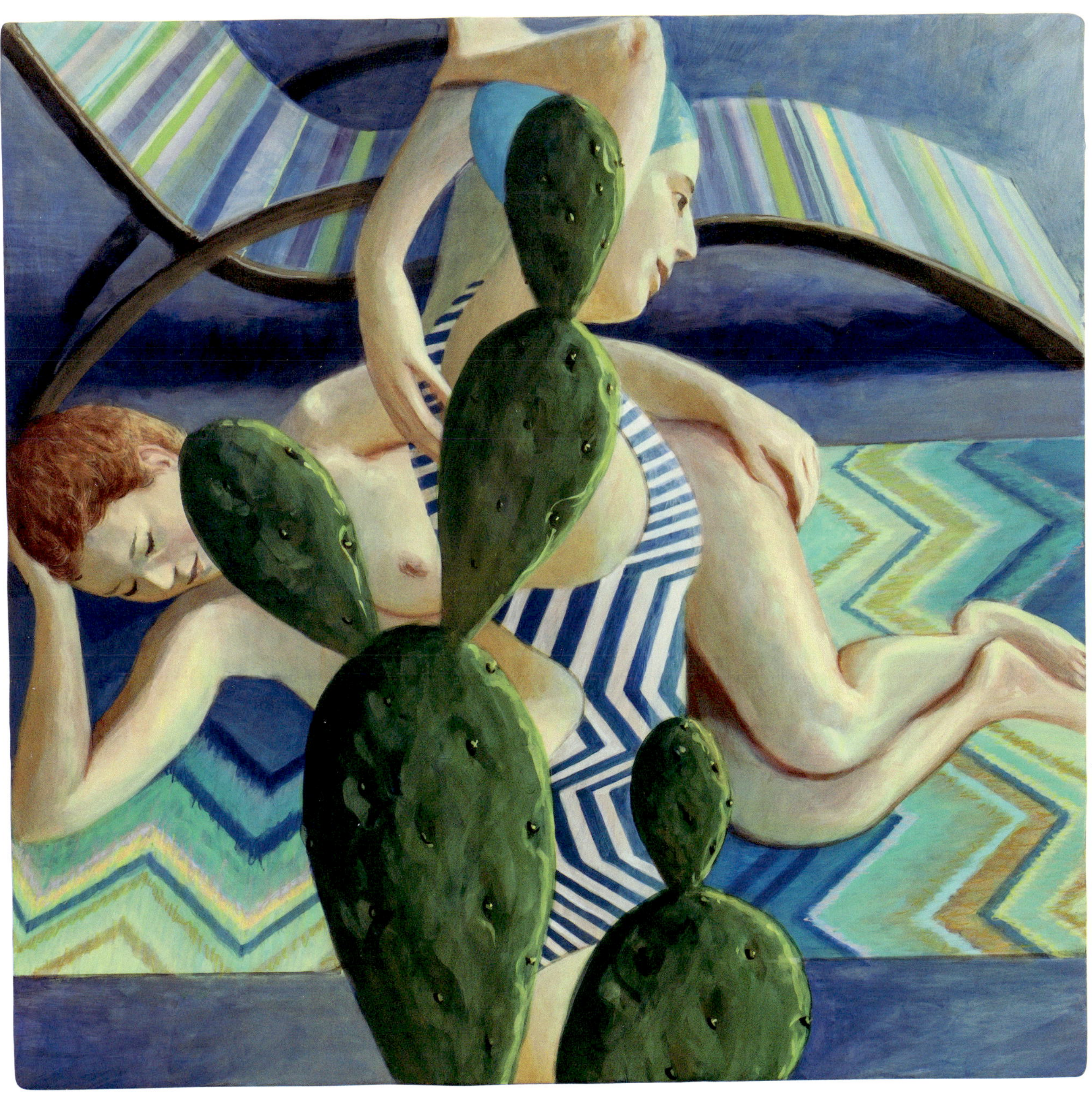

Orange Interior, 2013
Egg tempera on cotton on aluminium, 35 × 40 cm

Following spread:

Nature's Architecture (Gold), 2012
Egg tempera on cotton on aluminium, 45 × 70 cm

Nature's Architecture (Pink), 2012
Egg tempera on cotton on aluminium, 45 × 70 cm

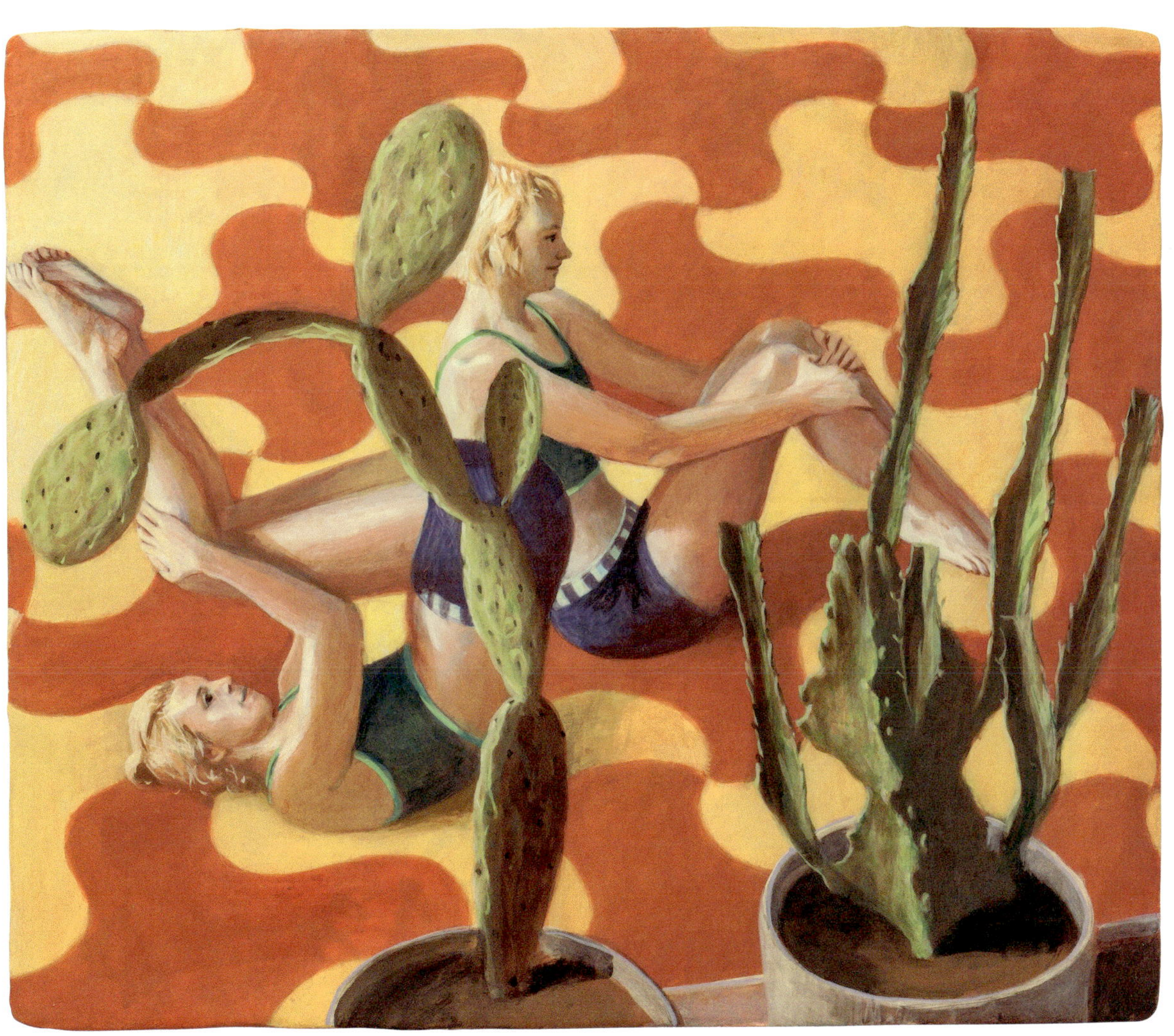

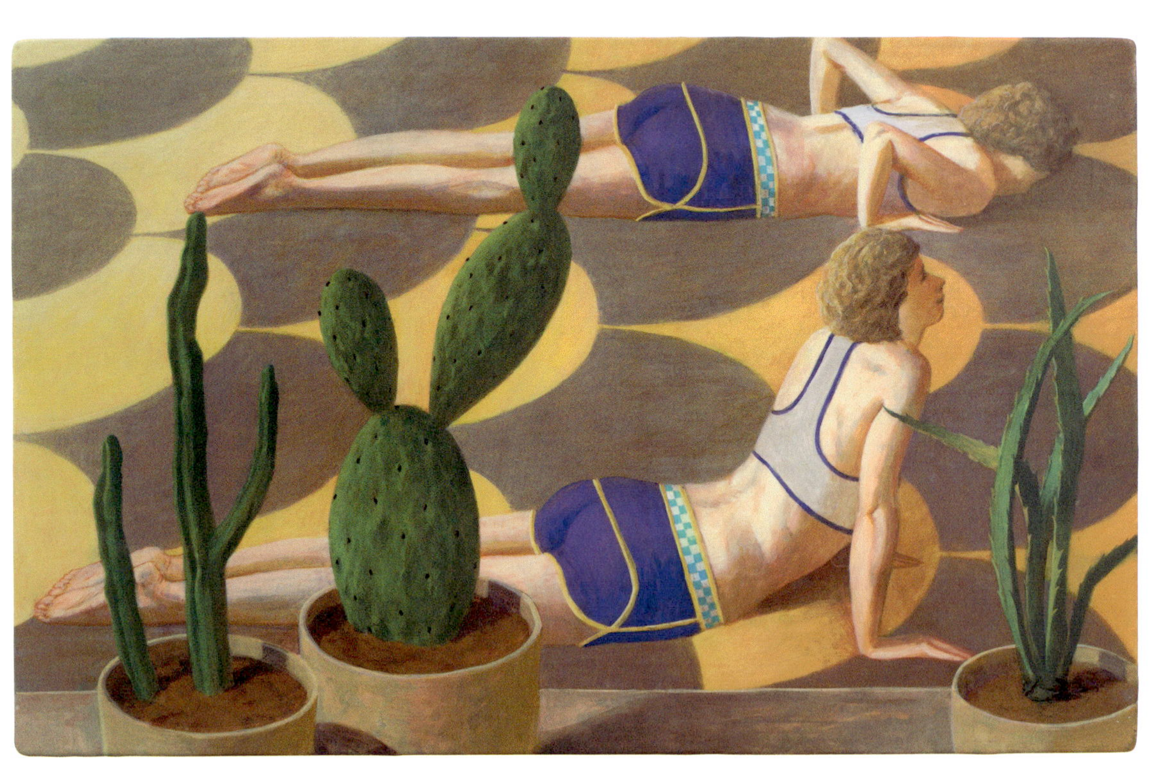

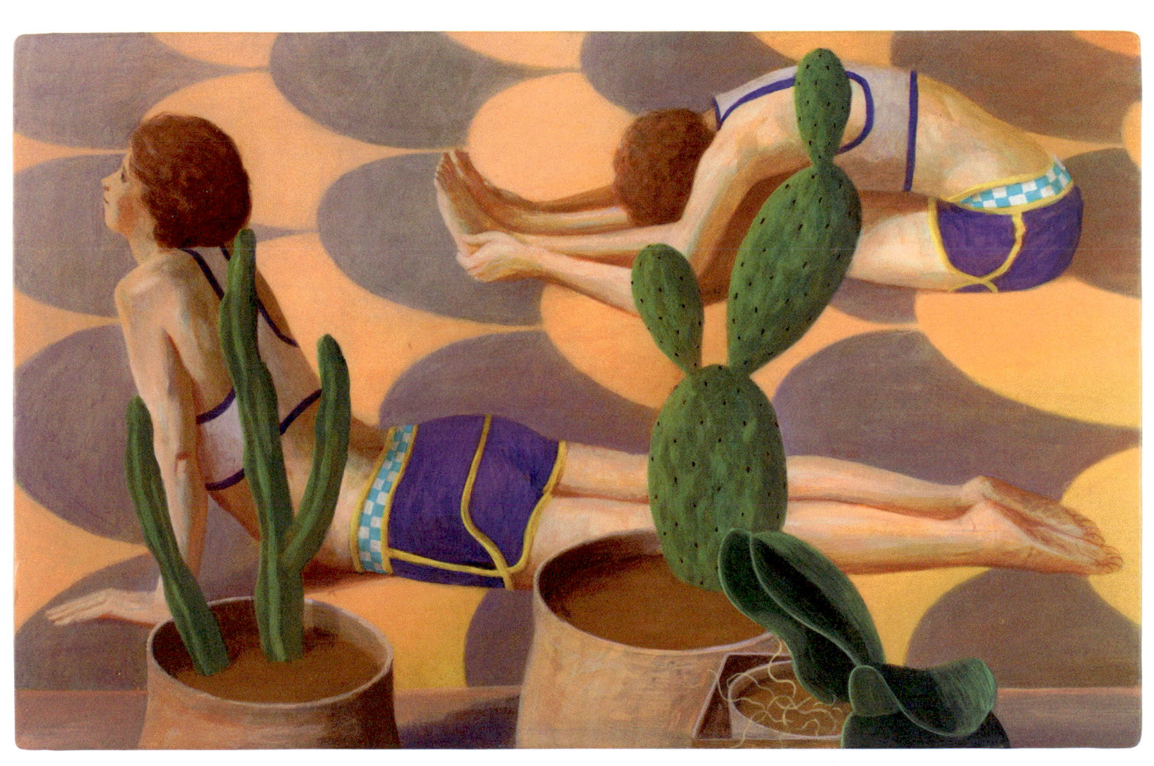

Yellow Interior with Cacti, 2013
Egg tempera on cotton on aluminium, 50 × 60 cm

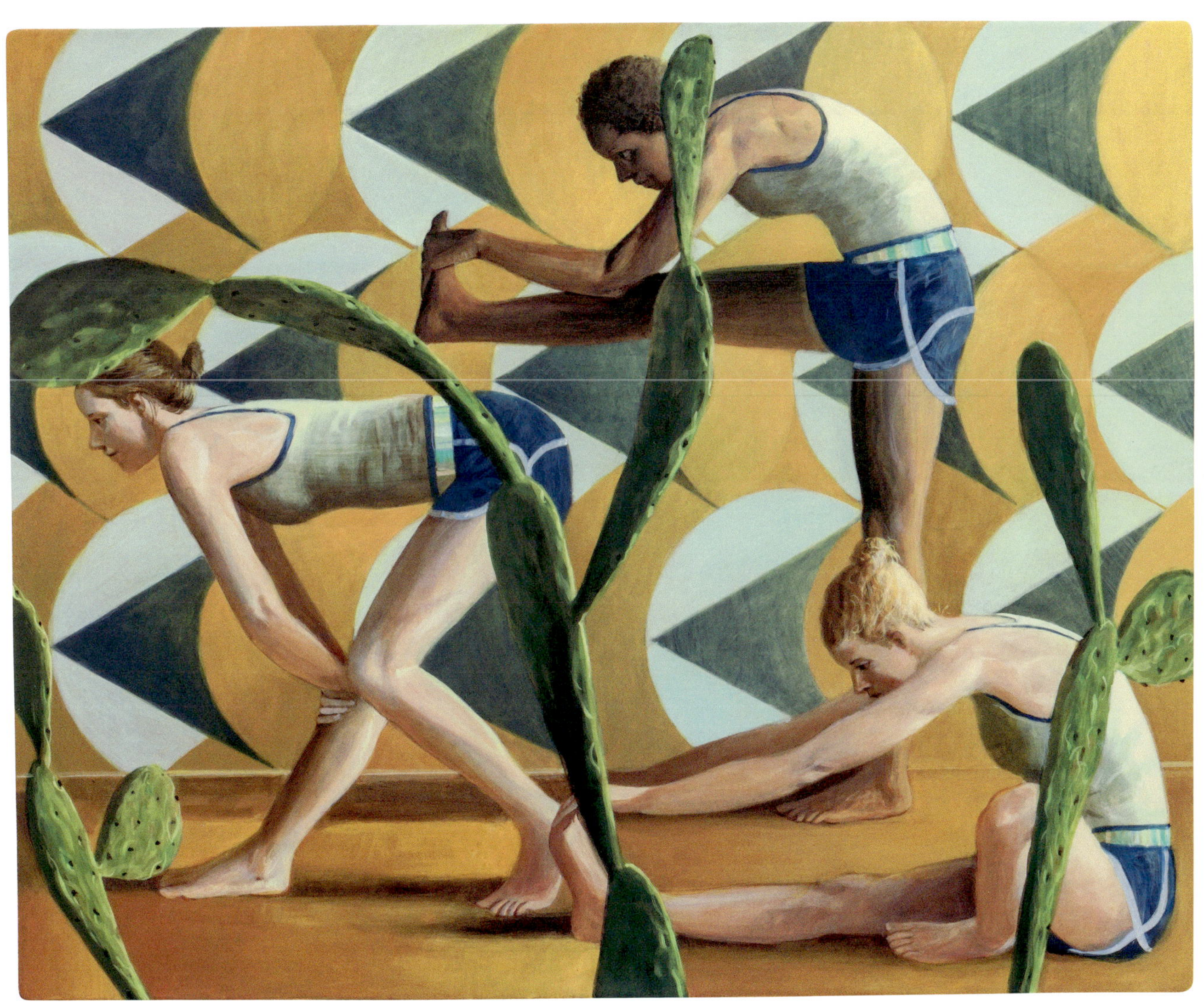

Ball Games I, 2013
Oil and egg tempera on linen, 50 × 70 cm

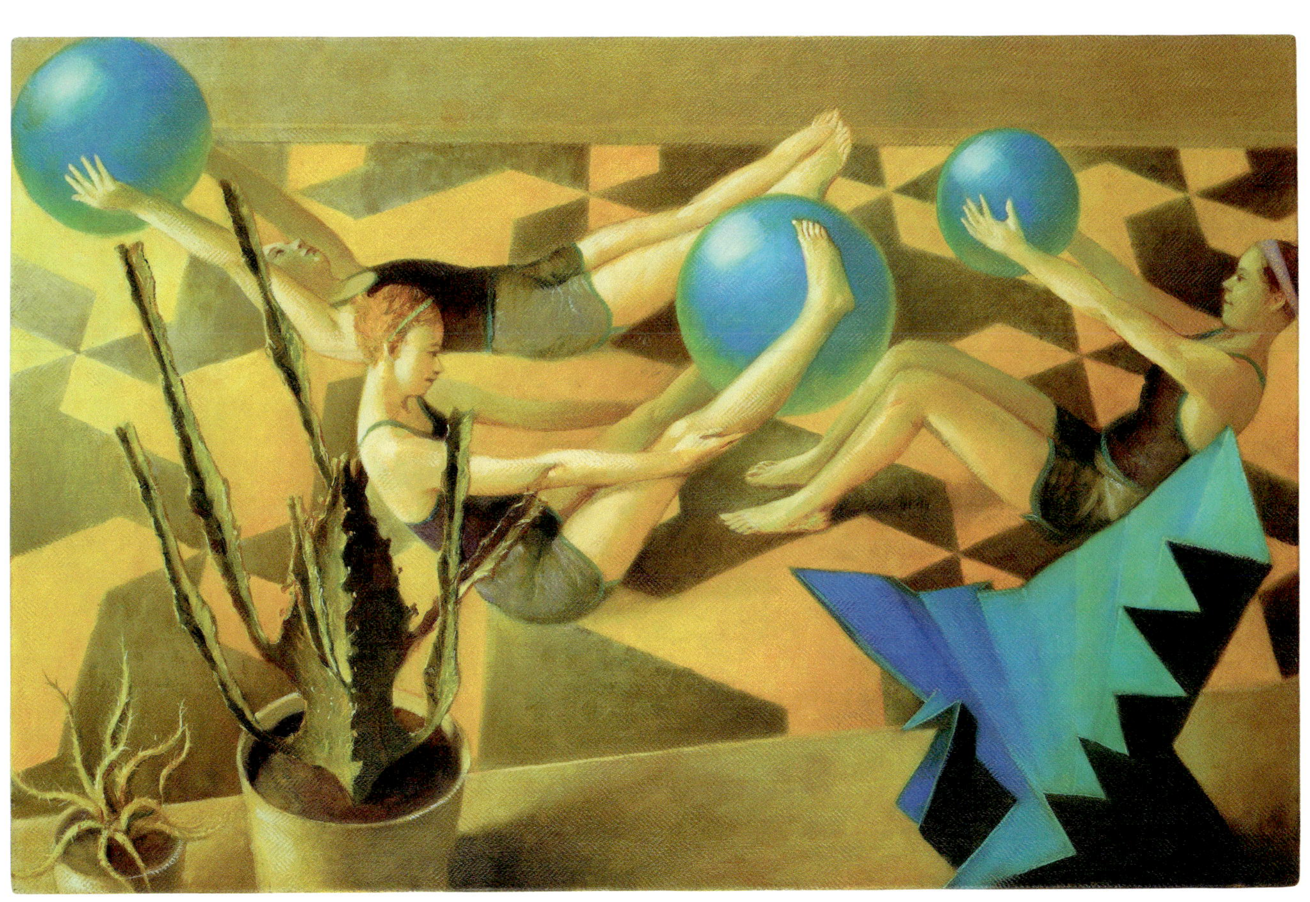

Ball Games II, 2013
Oil and egg tempera on linen, 46 × 36 cm

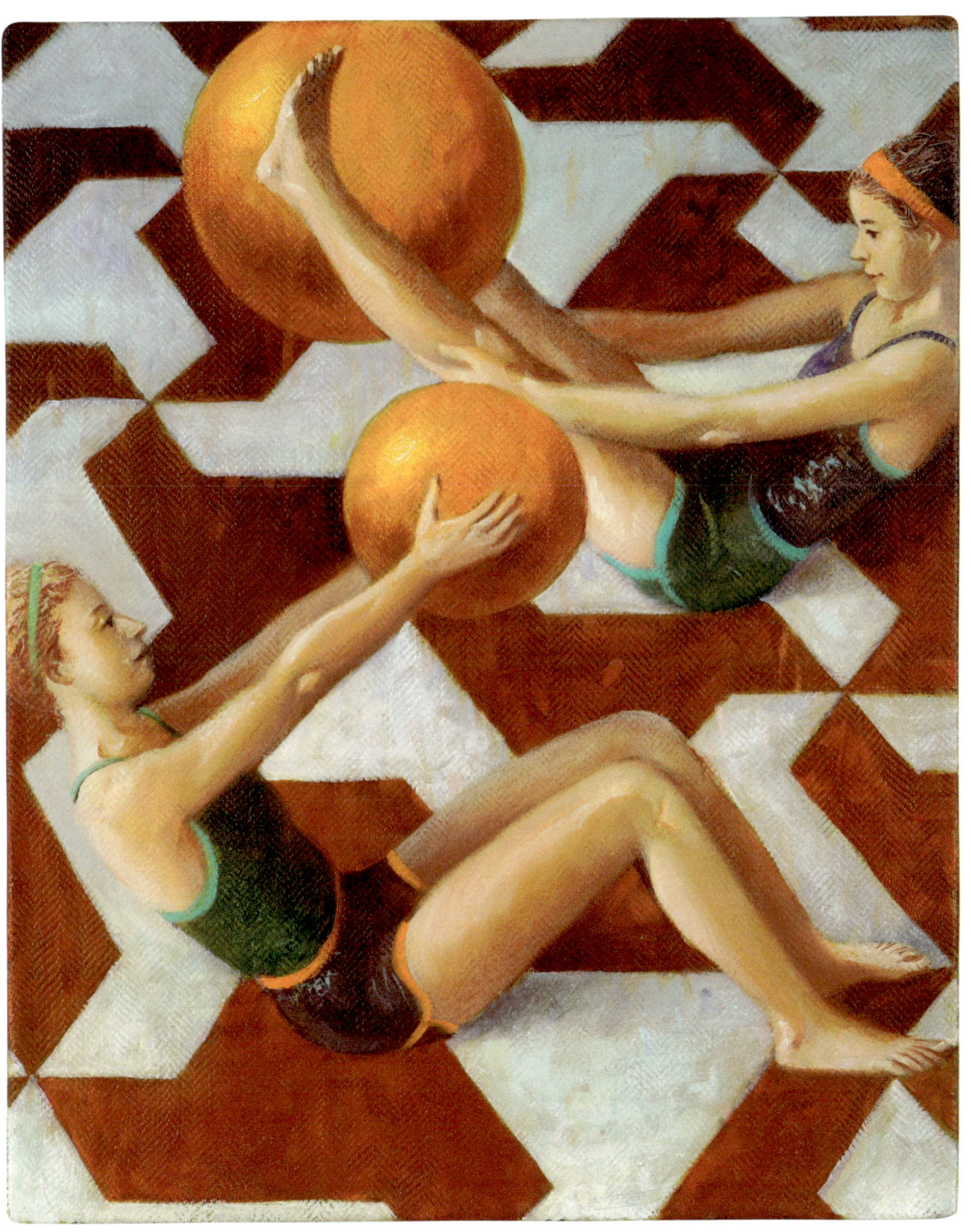

Ball Games III, 2013
Oil and egg tempera on linen, 70 × 100 cm

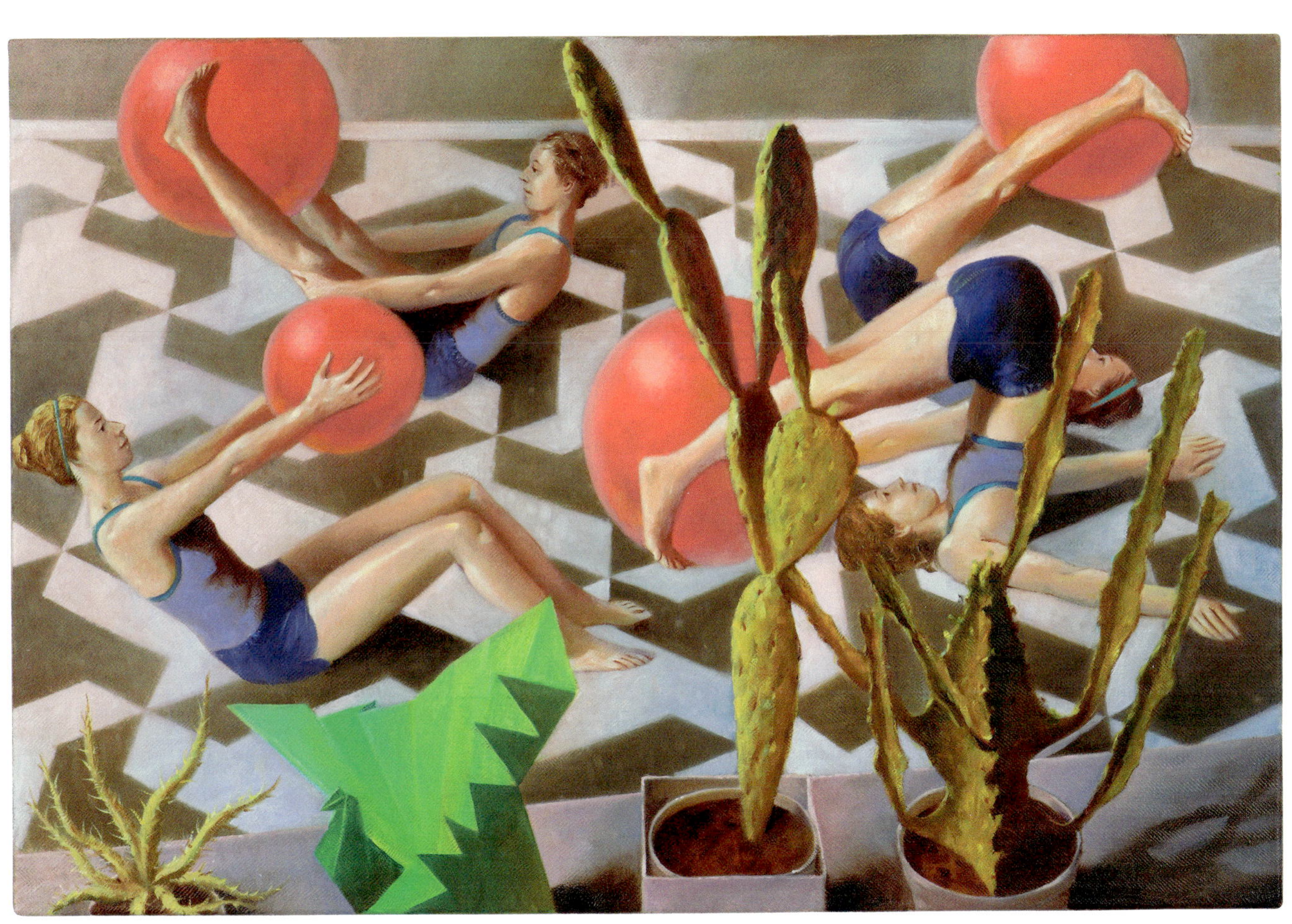

Ball Games IV, 2013
Oil and egg tempera on linen, 50 × 75 cm

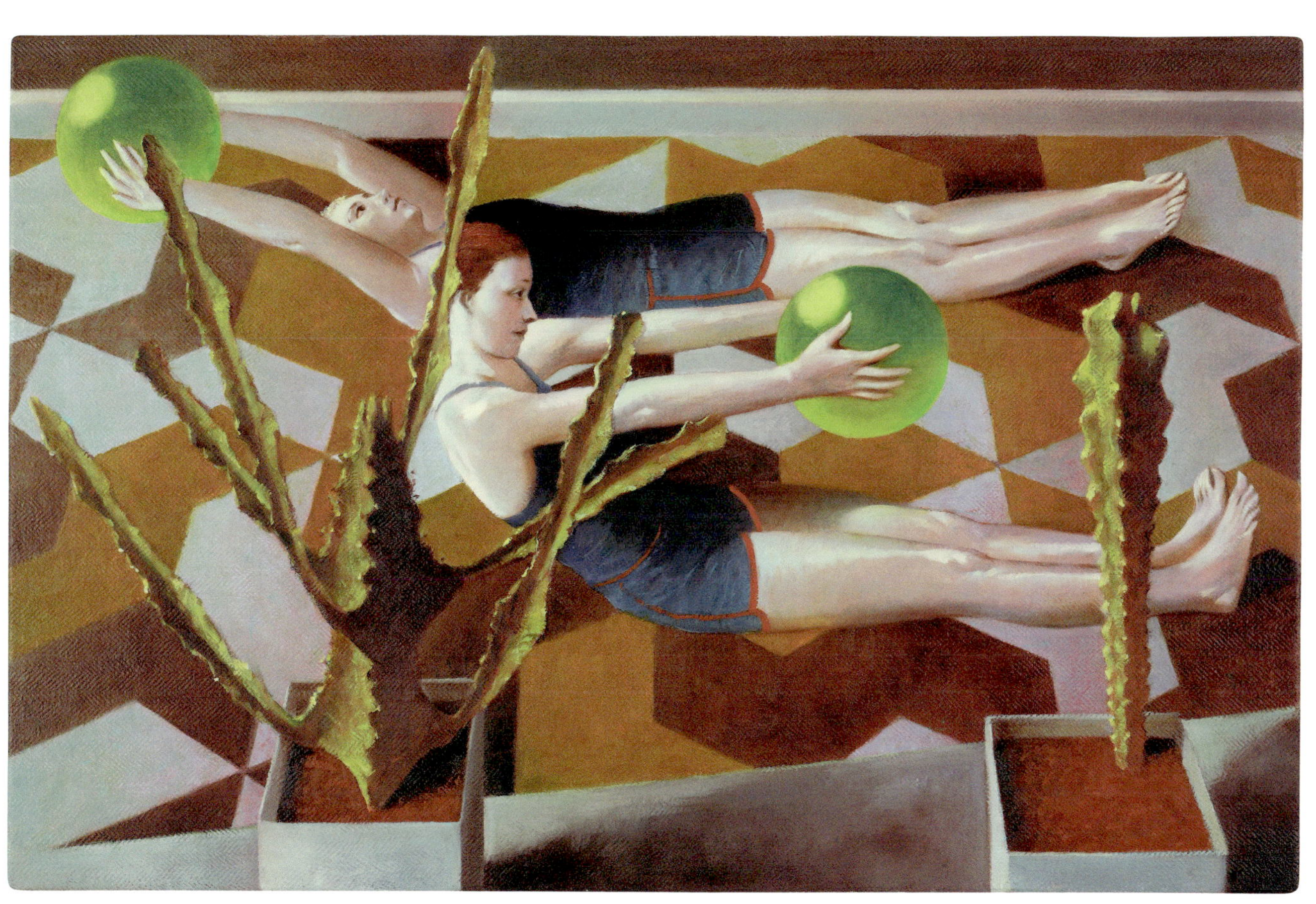

Rings IV (Autumn), 2014
Egg tempera on linen on plywood, 60 × 40 cm

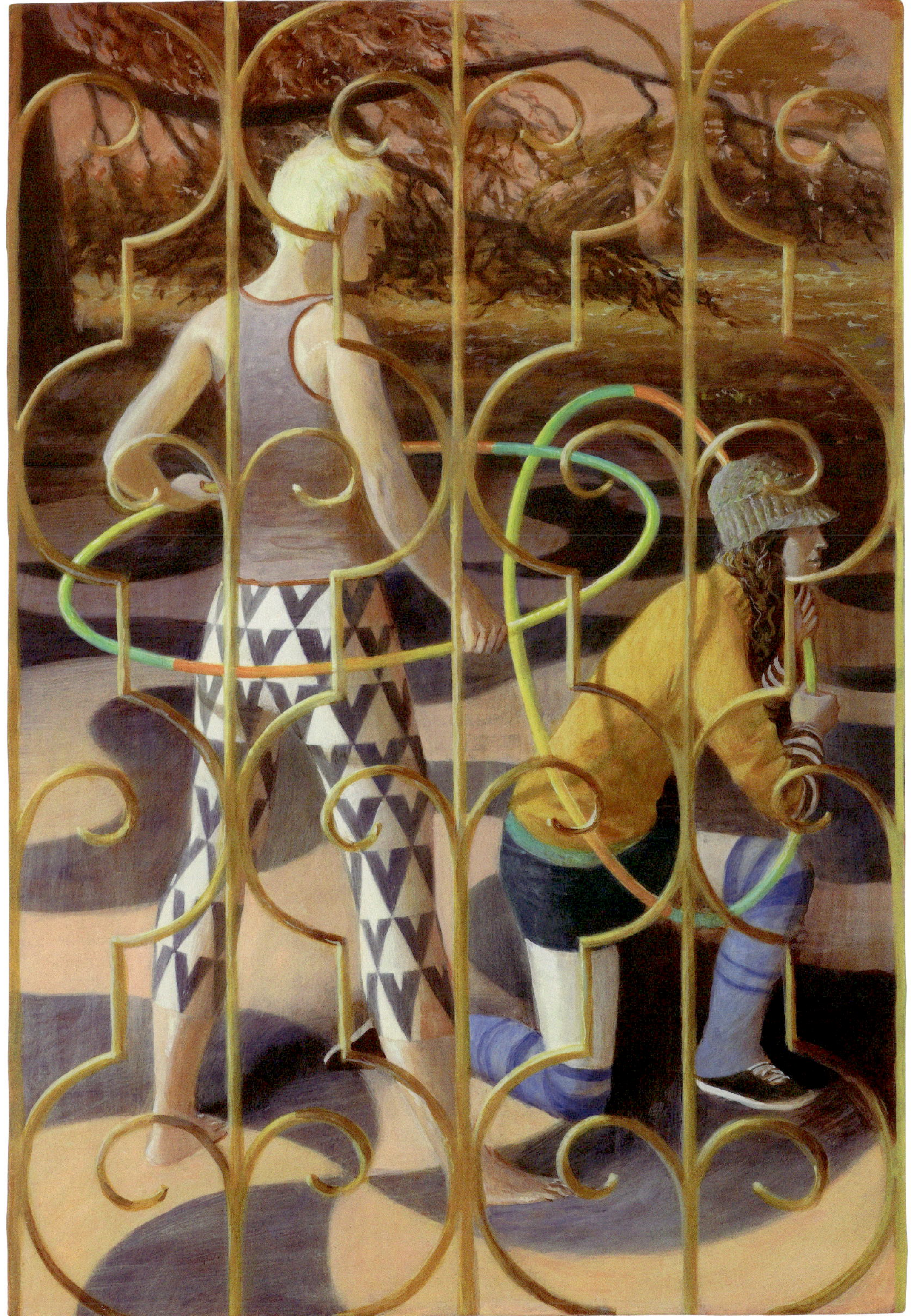

Rings V (Cartwheels), 2014
Egg tempera on linen on plywood, 40 × 60 cm

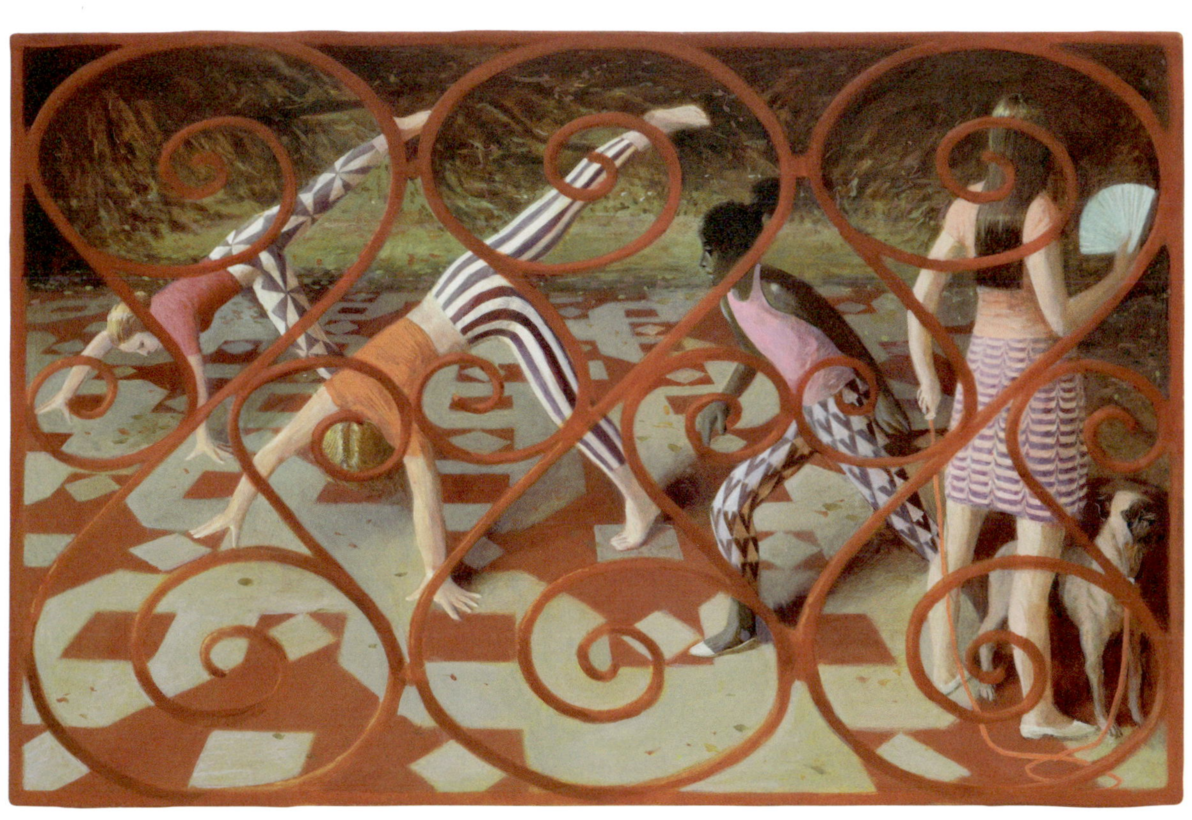

Rings VII (Light and Distance), 2014
Egg tempera on cotton on plywood, 60 × 50 cm

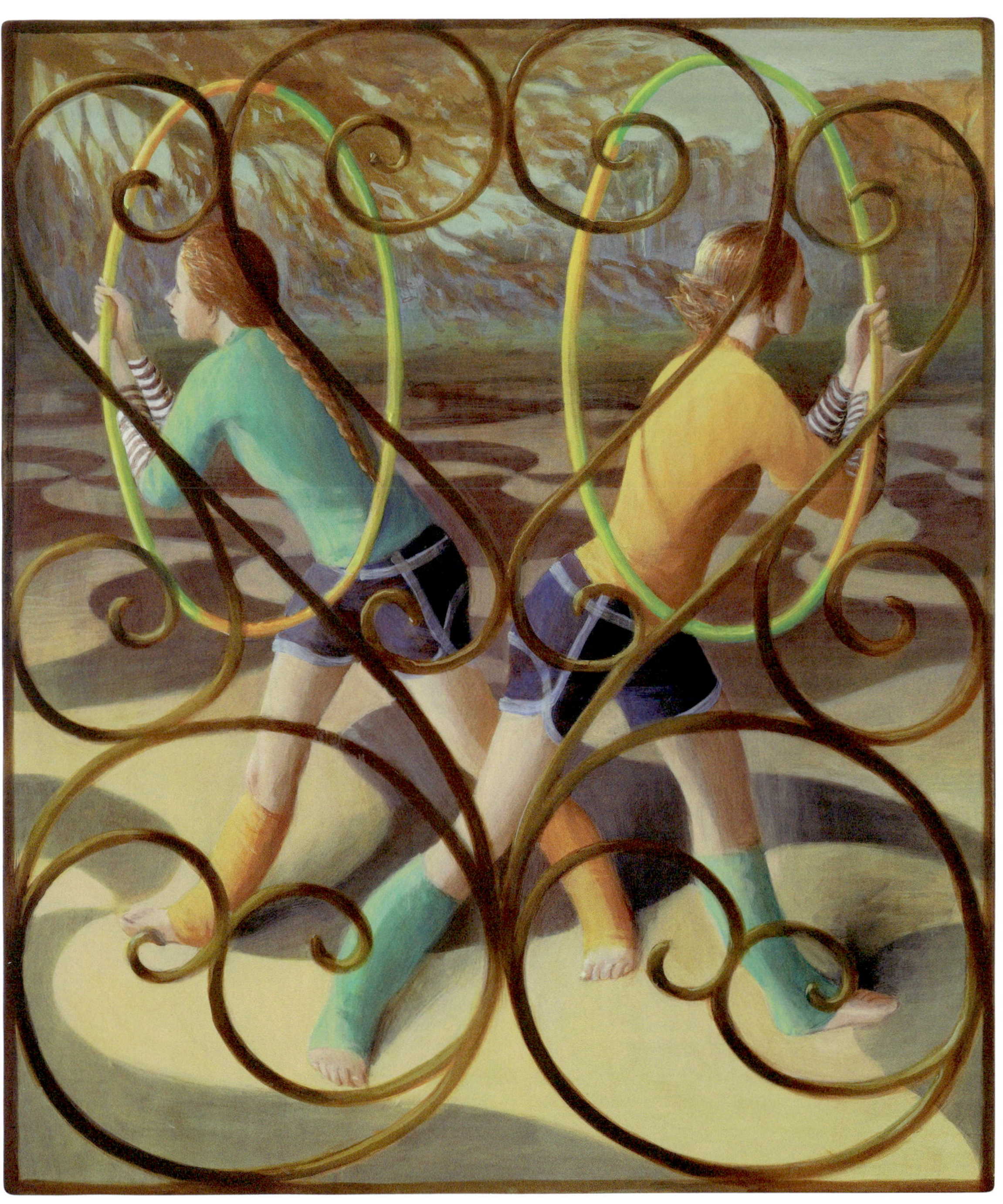

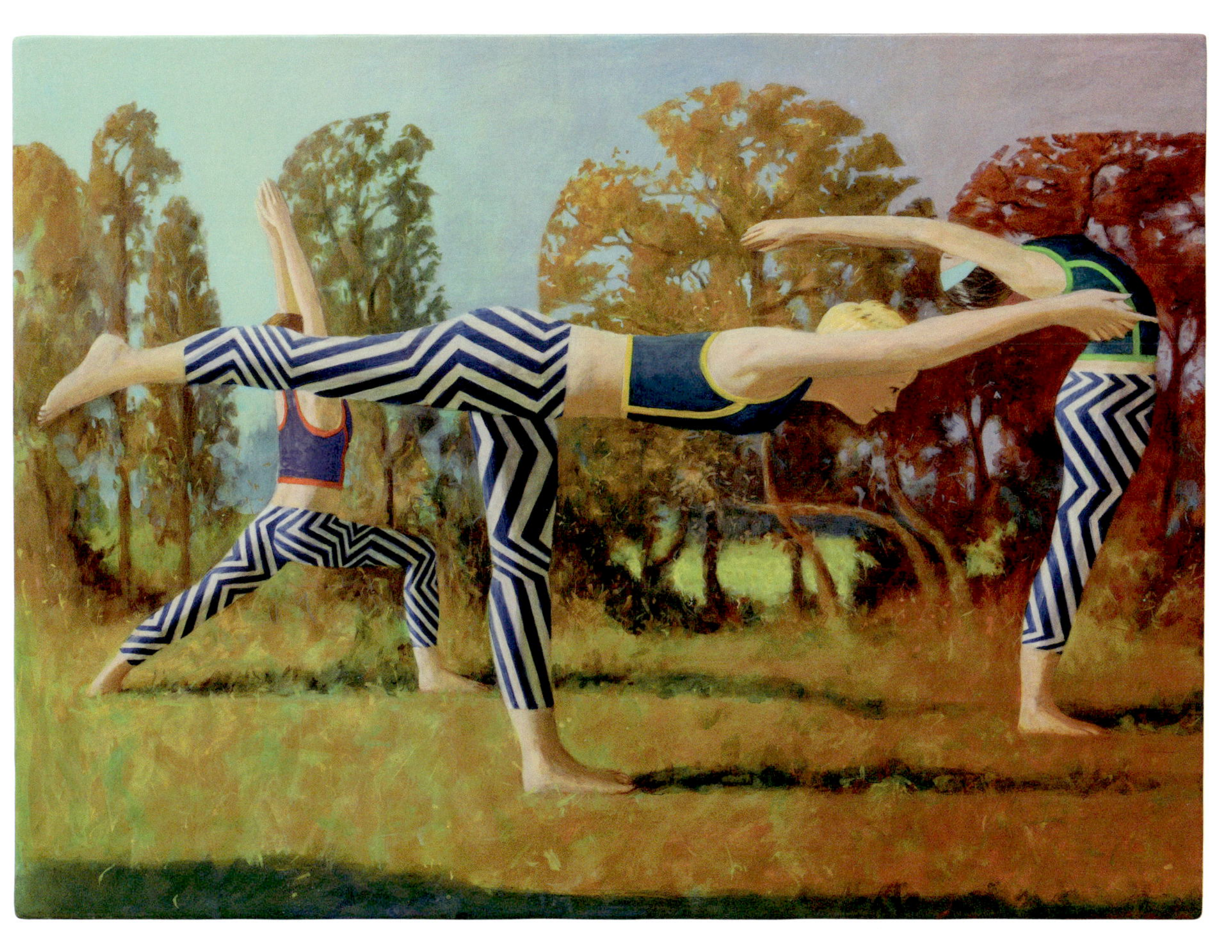

Westerly, 2014
Oil on linen, 51 × 76 cm

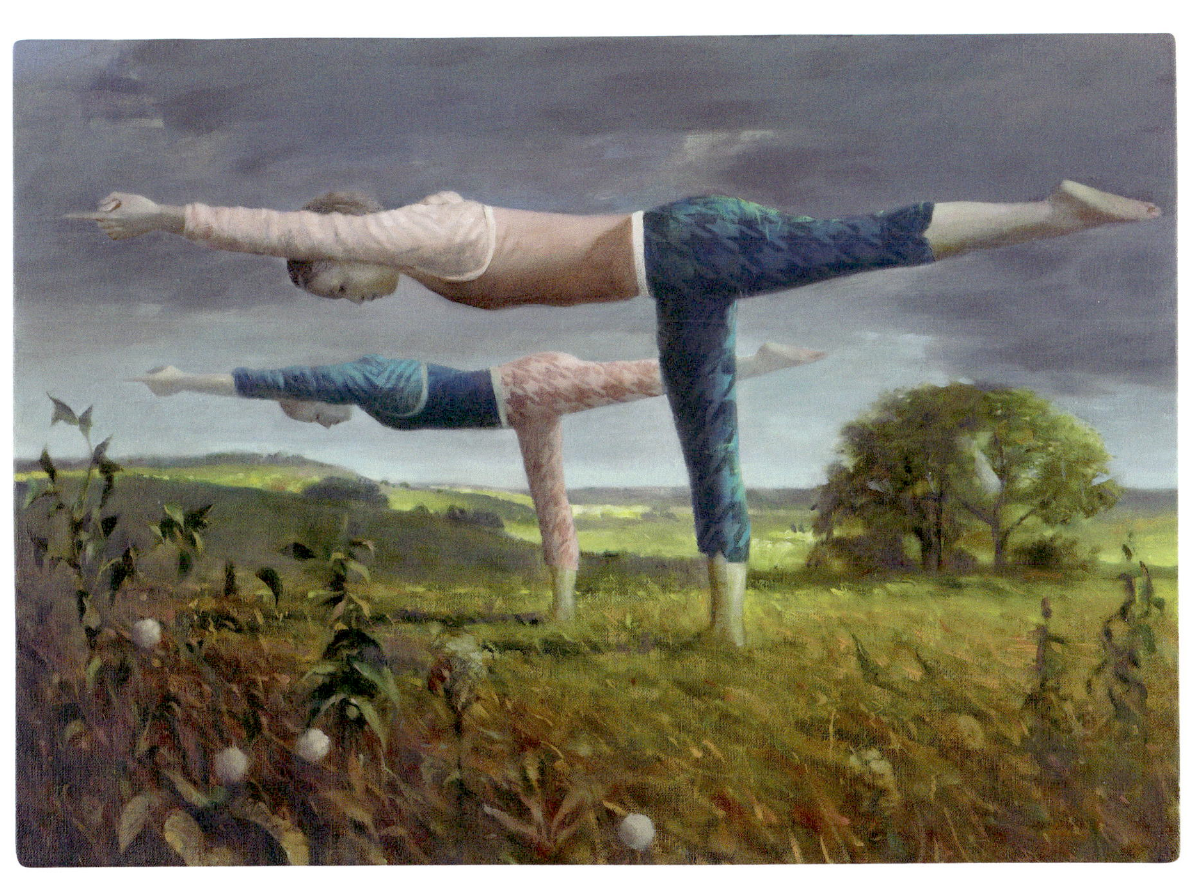

Birth of Spring (Tondo), 2013
Egg tempera on cotton on aluminium, ⌀60 cm

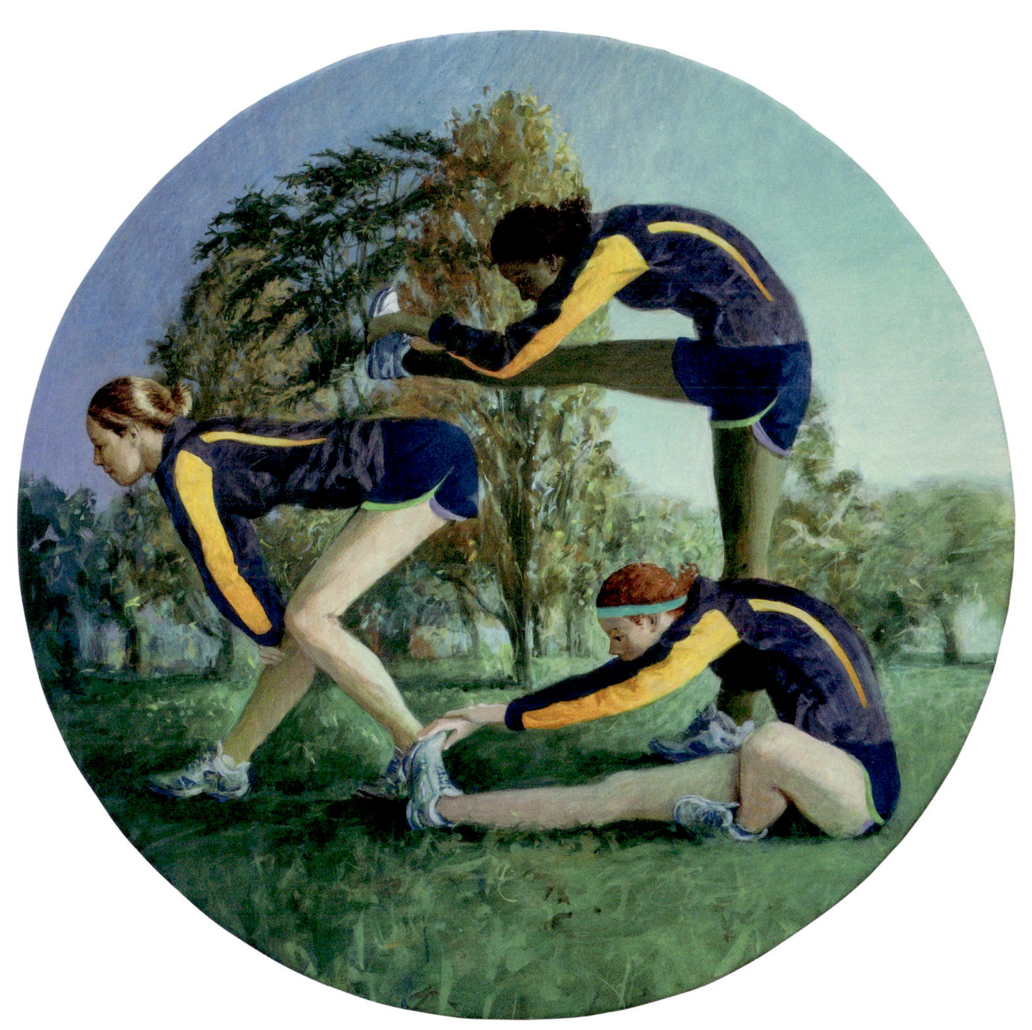

Beacon Hill, 2014
Oil on linen, 100 × 150 cm

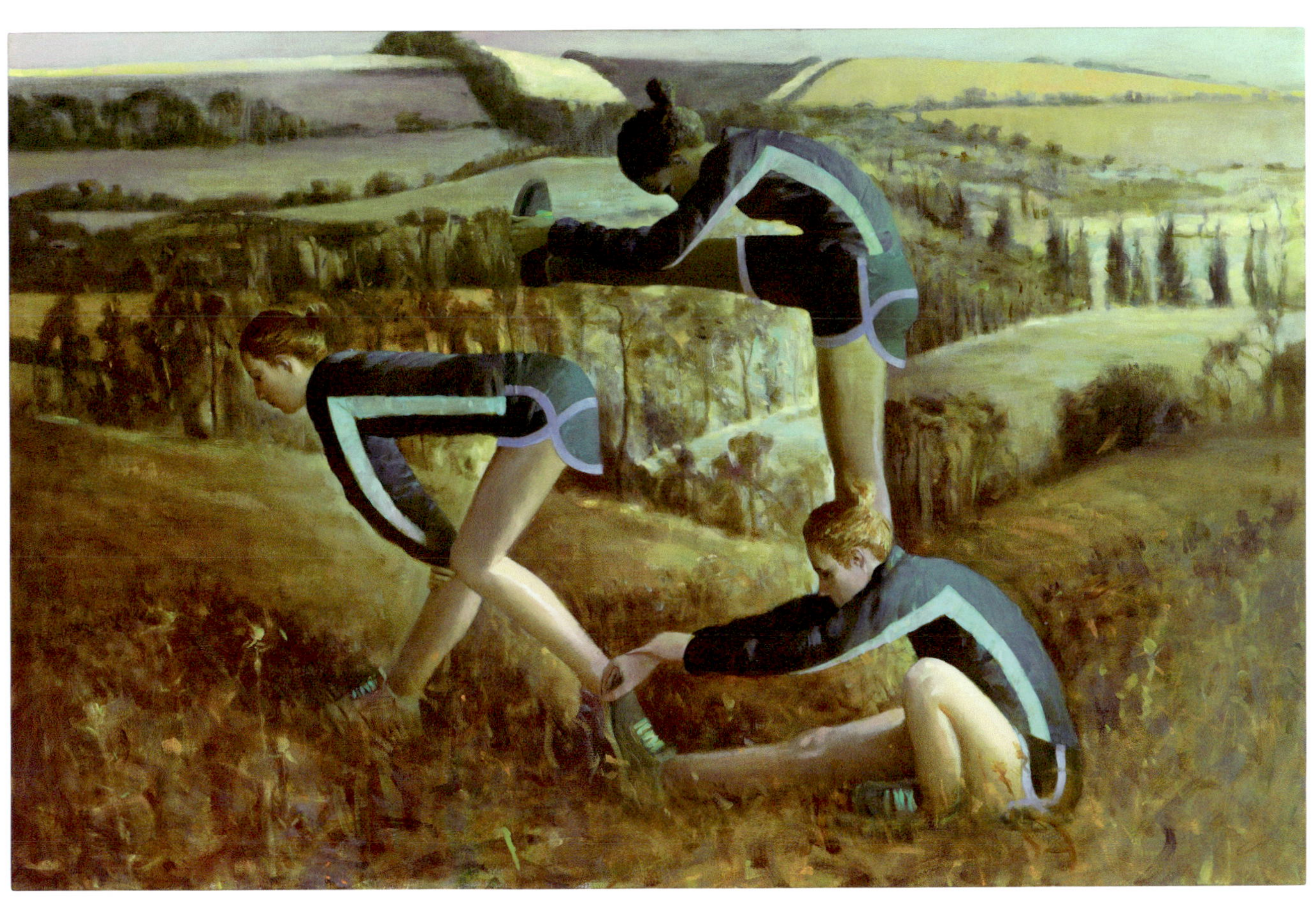

On Dark Hill, 2013
Egg tempera on cotton on aluminium, 60 × 60 cm

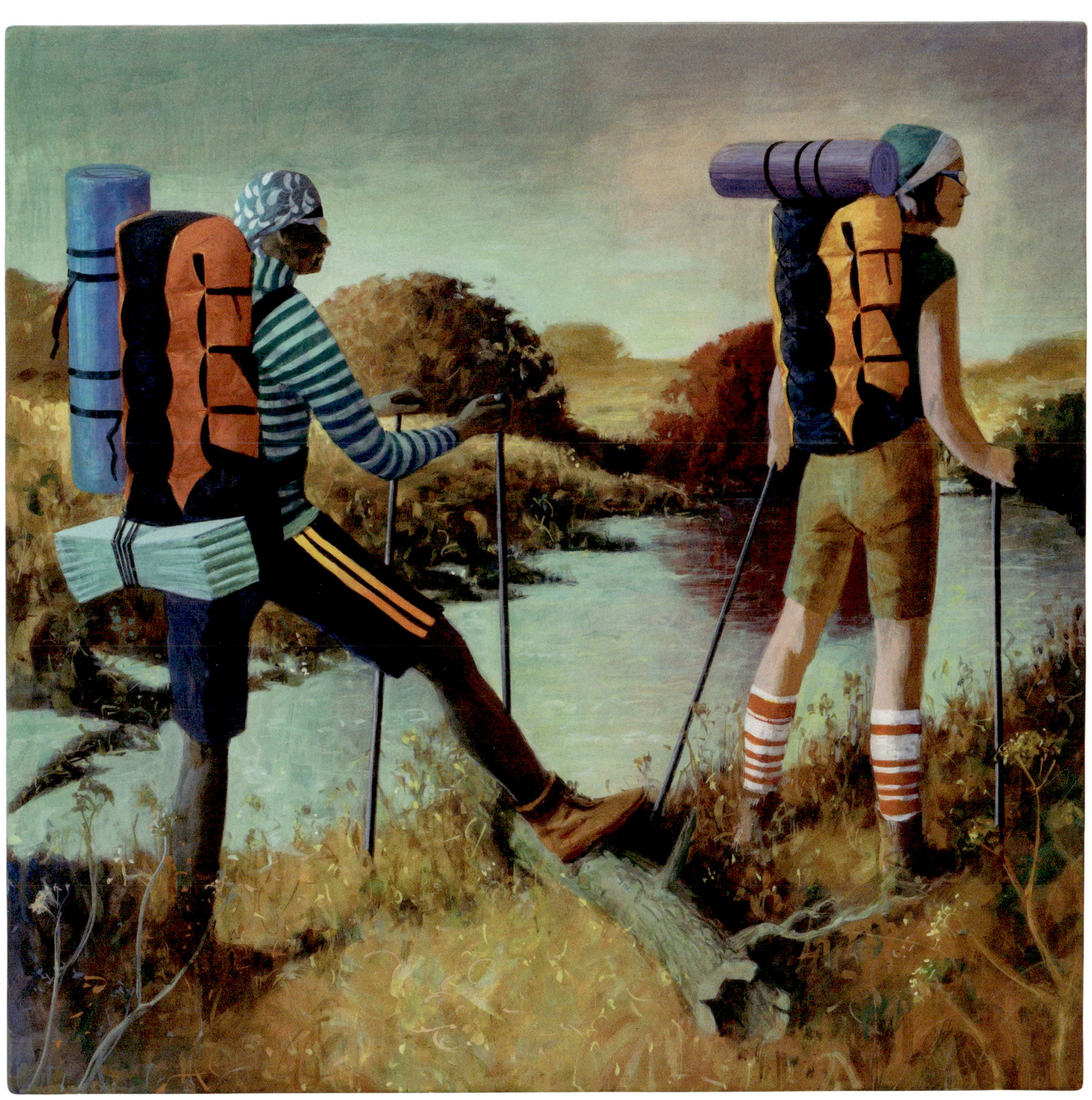

Three Walkers on Beacon Hill (Spring), 2014
Oil on linen, 80 × 100 cm

Following spread:

The Walker, 2014
Oil on linen, 36 × 25 cm

Two Walkers on Ladle Hill, 2014
Oil on linen, 36 × 32 cm

78

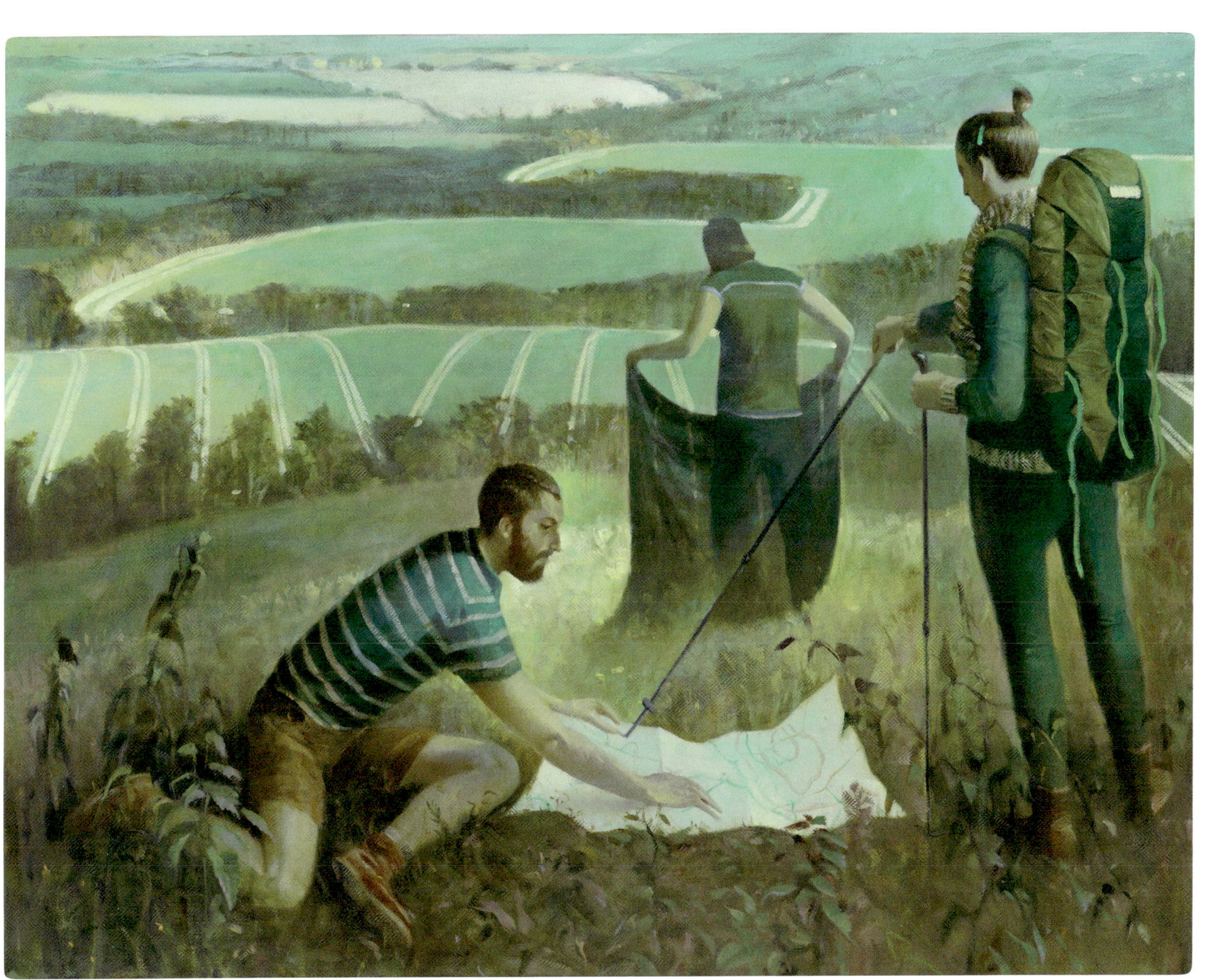

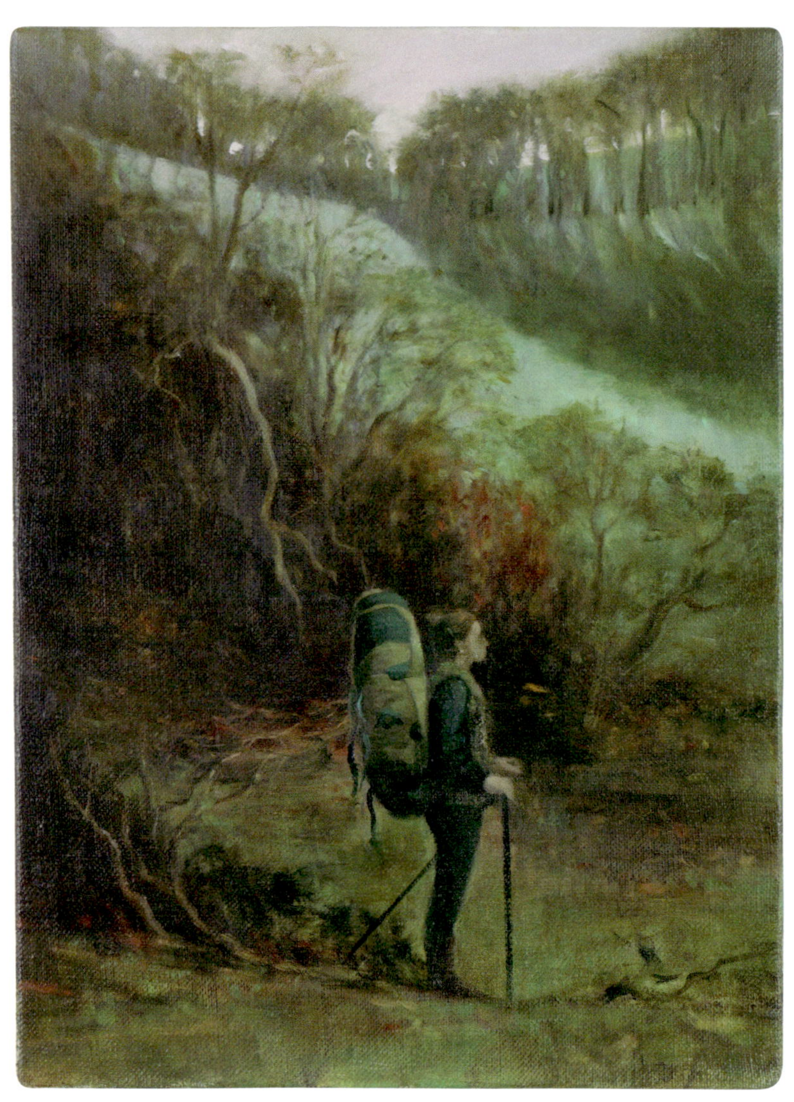

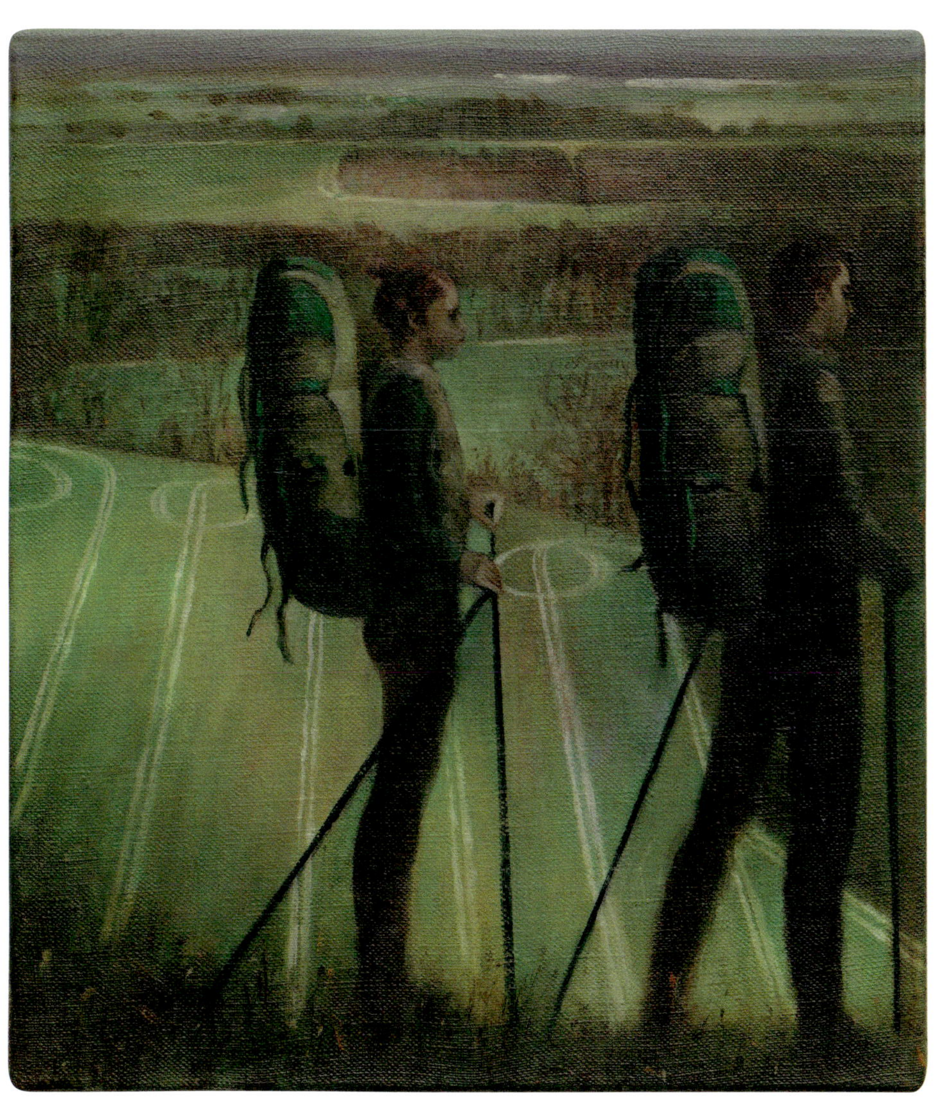

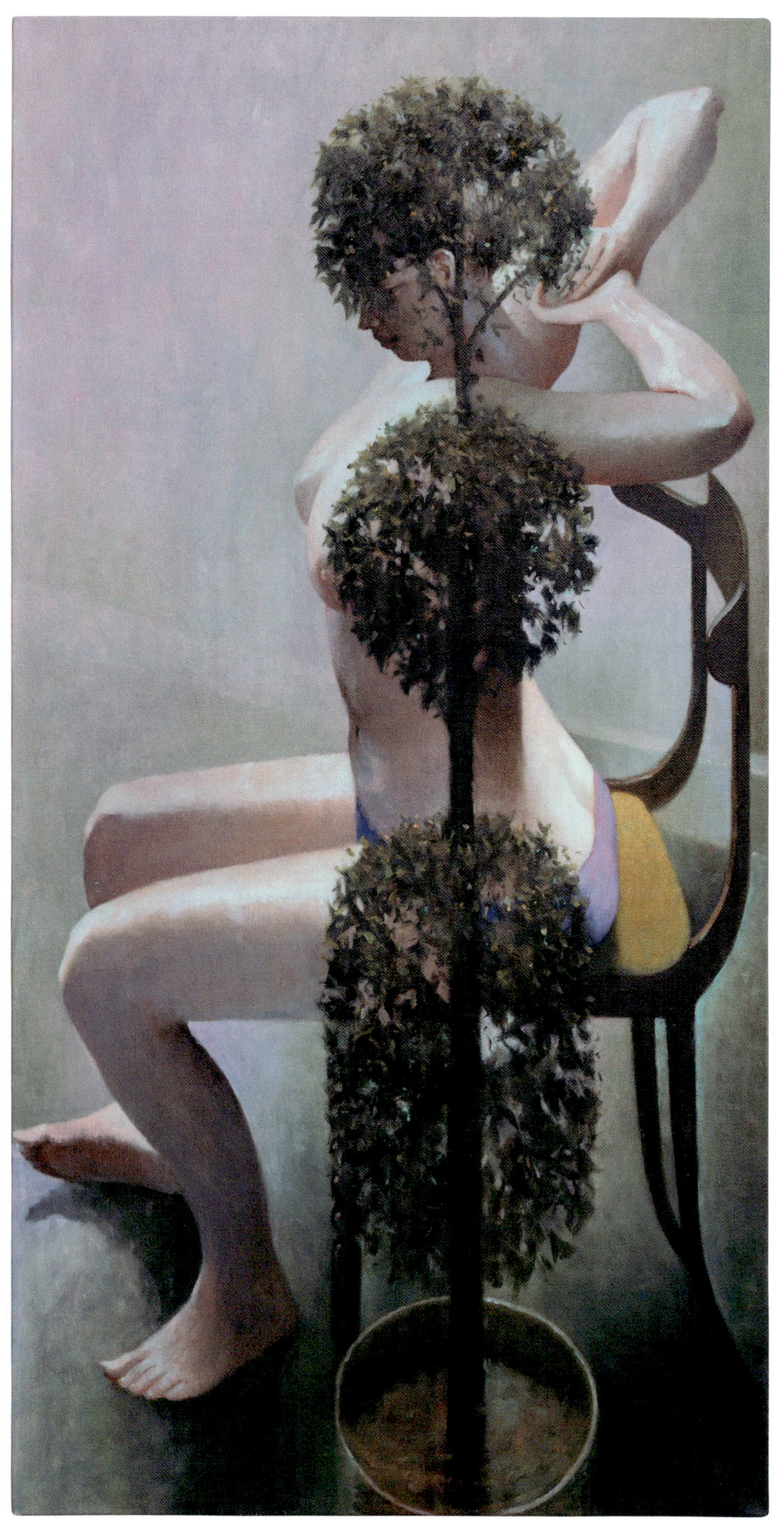

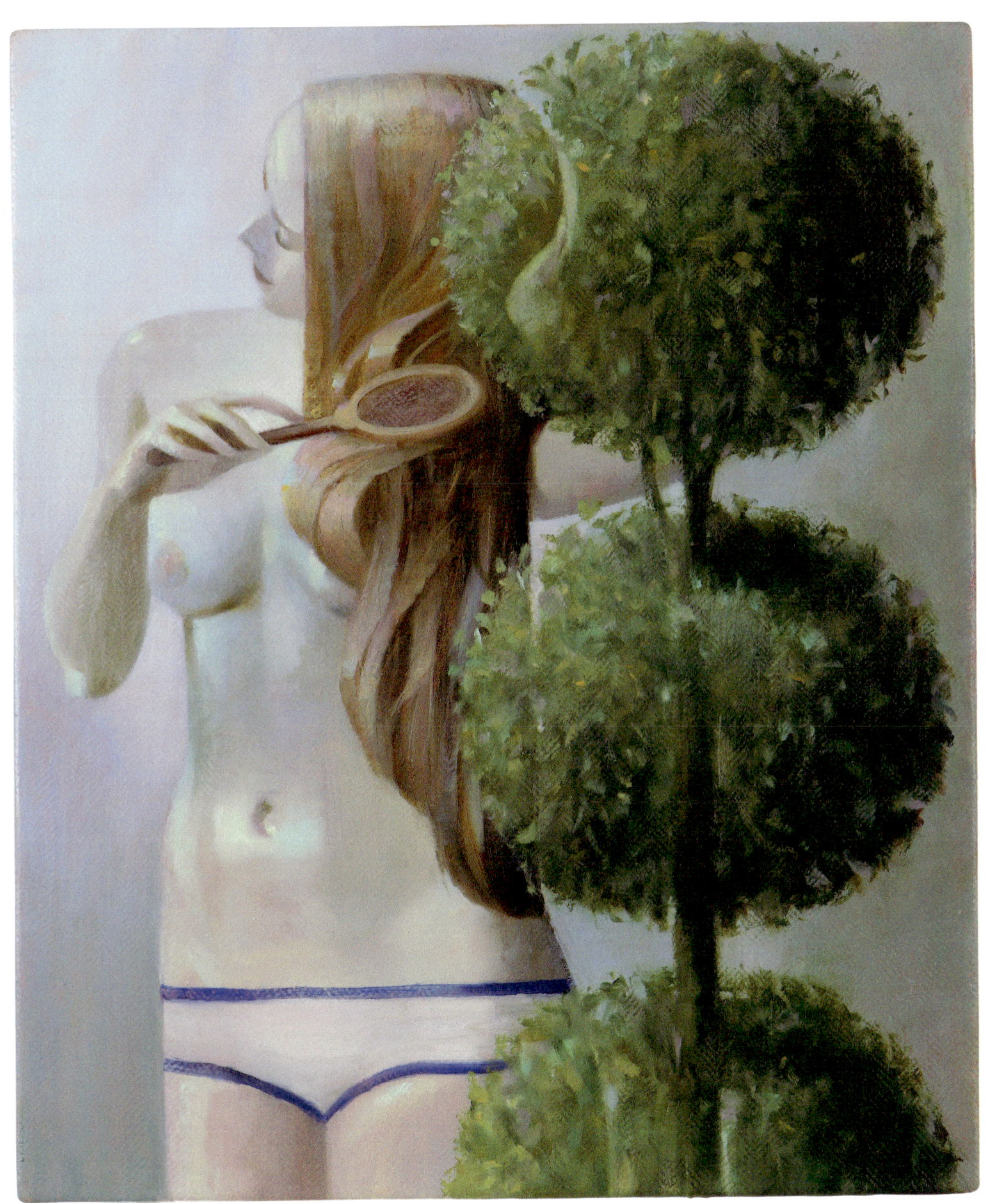

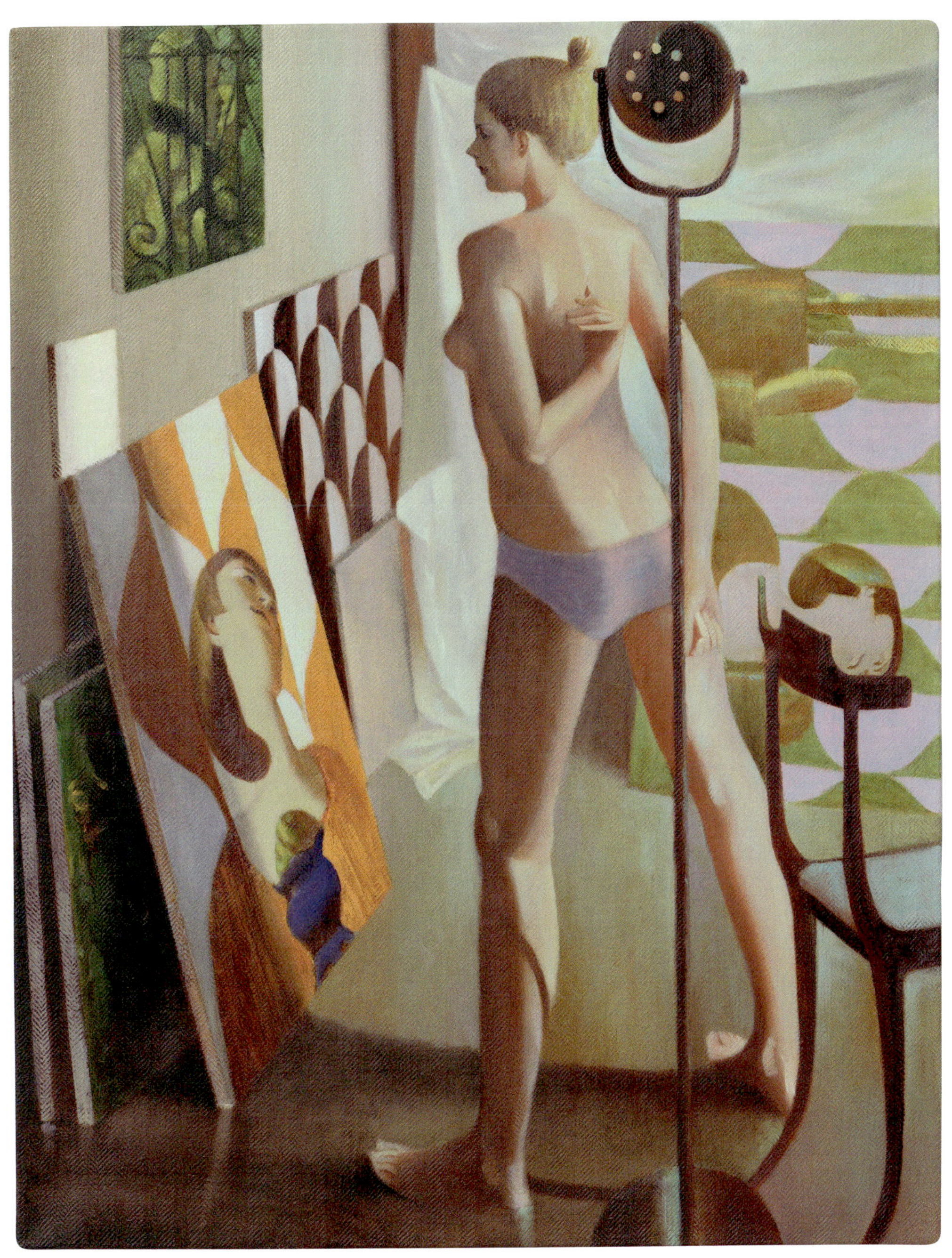

Dogtooth Dog Walker, 2015
Oil on linen, 150 × 100 cm

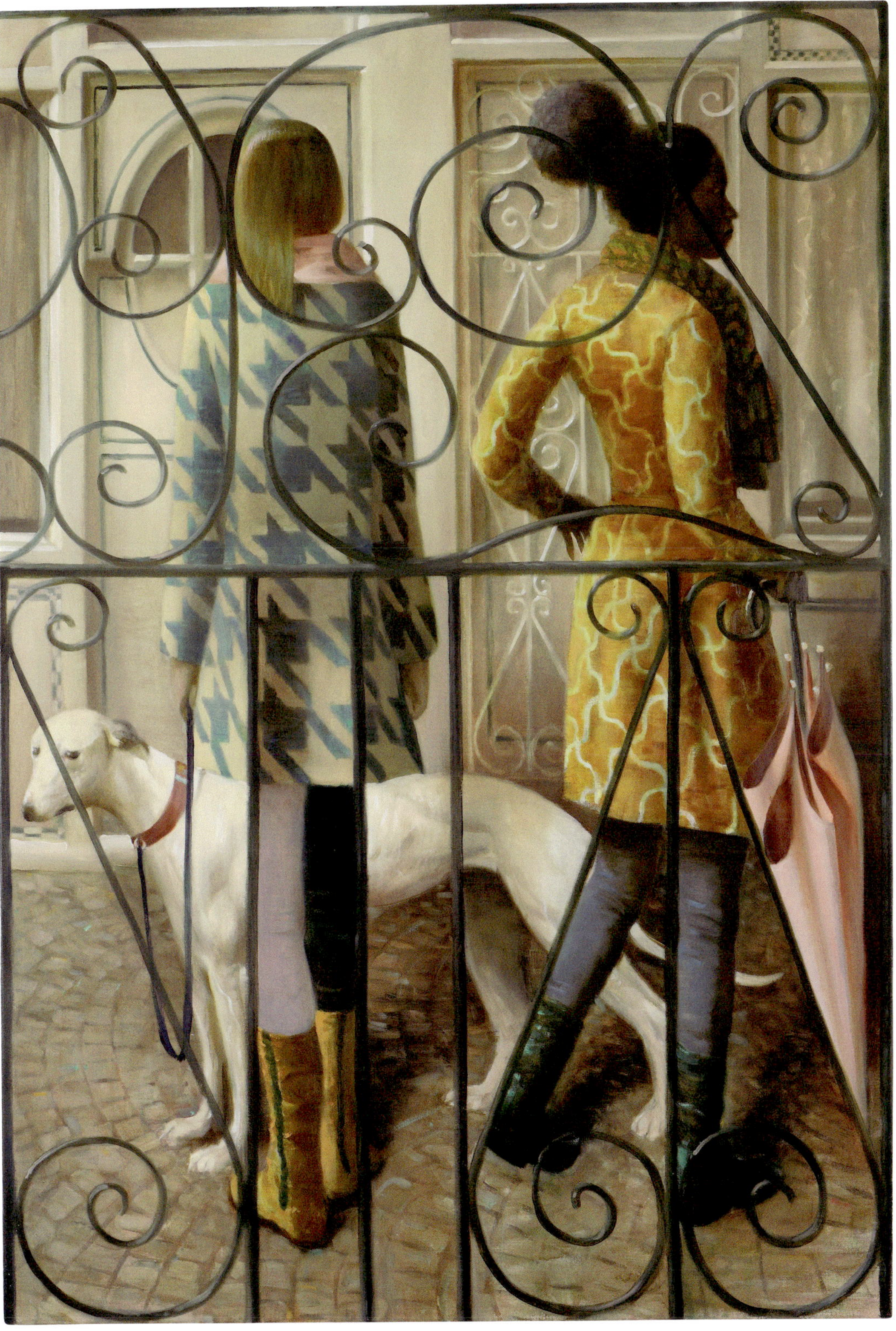

Dogtooth III, 2014
Oil on linen, 61 × 51 cm

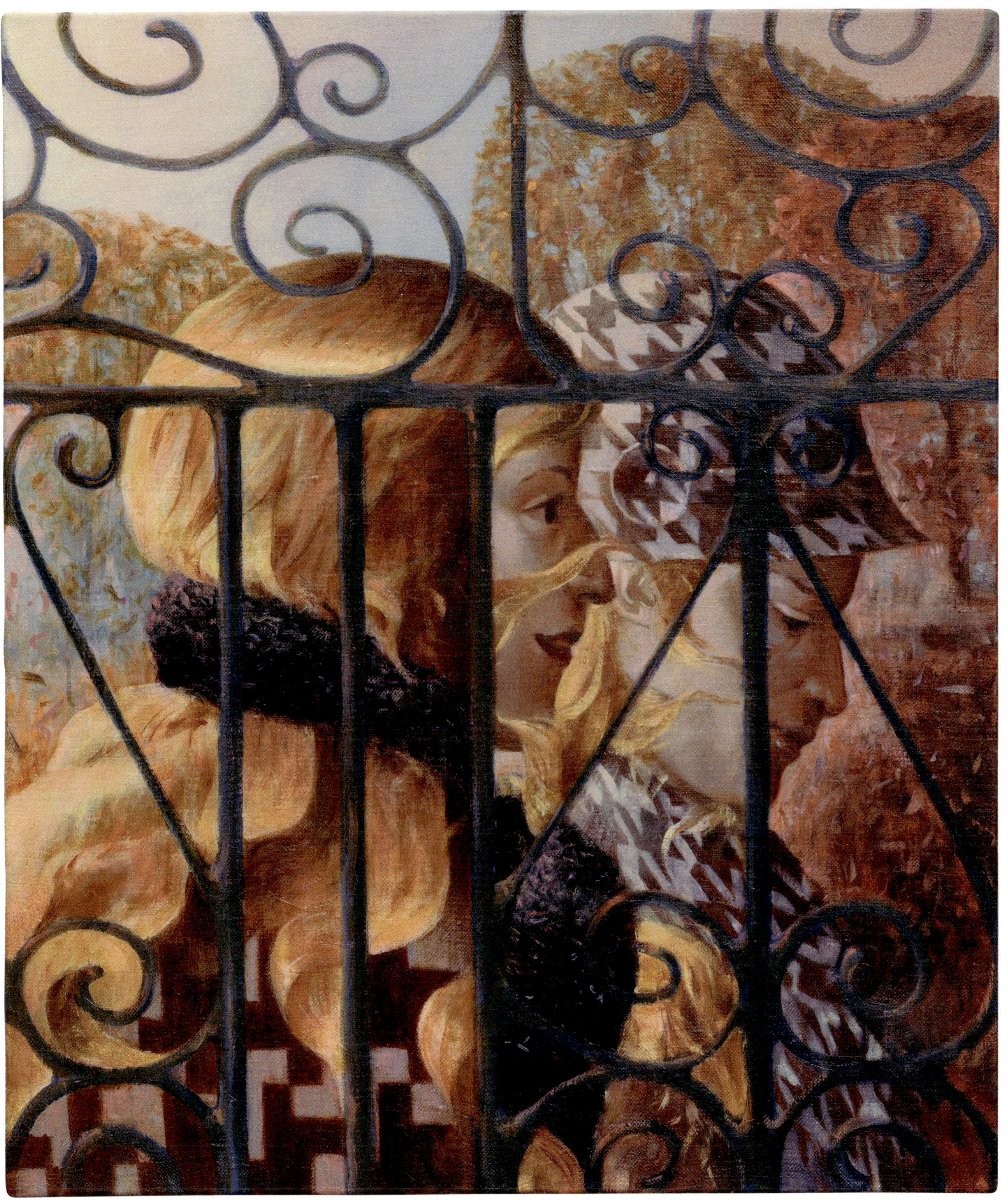

Green Shop, 2015
Oil on linen, 76 × 51 cm

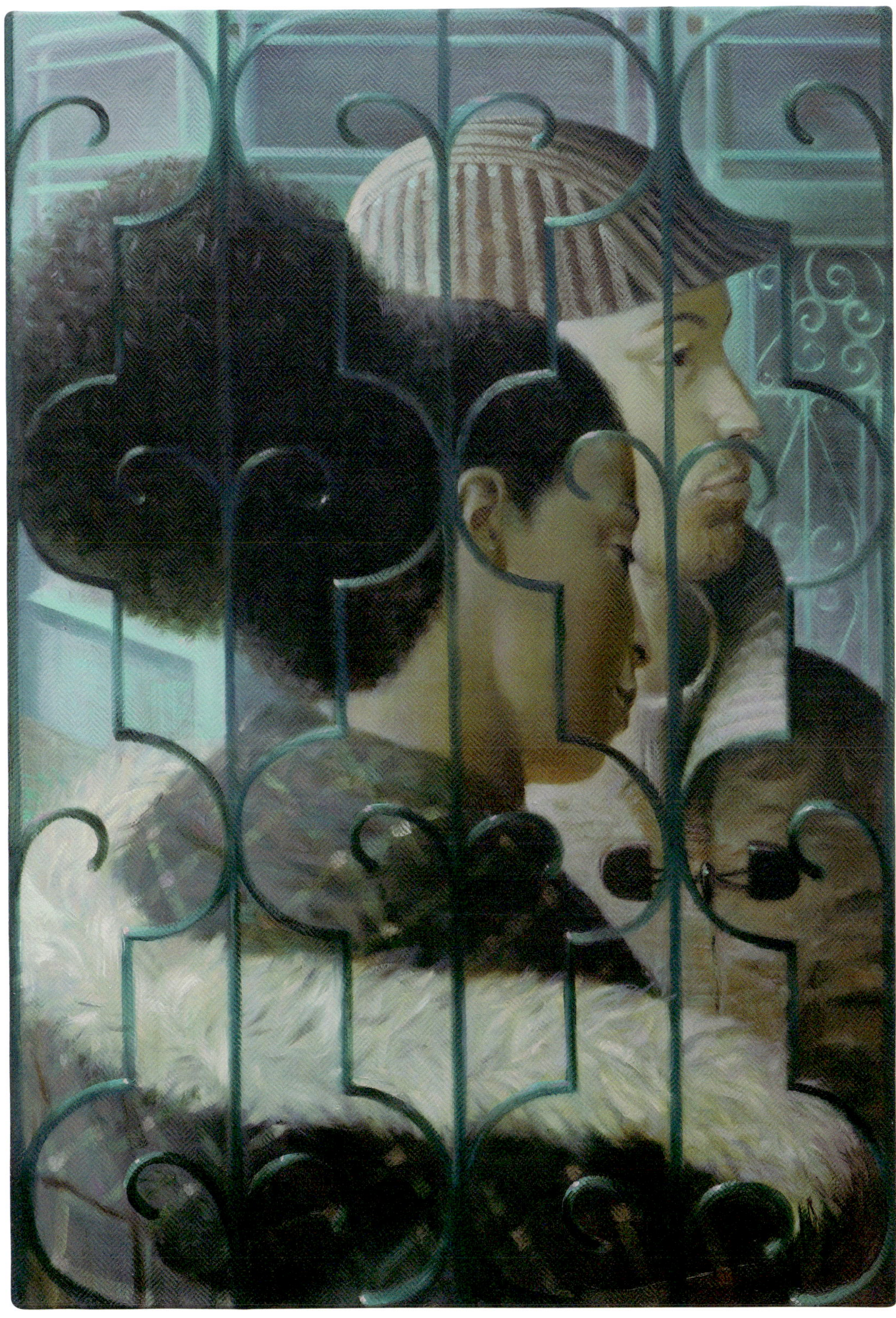

Commuters, 2014
Oil on linen, 66 × 86 cm

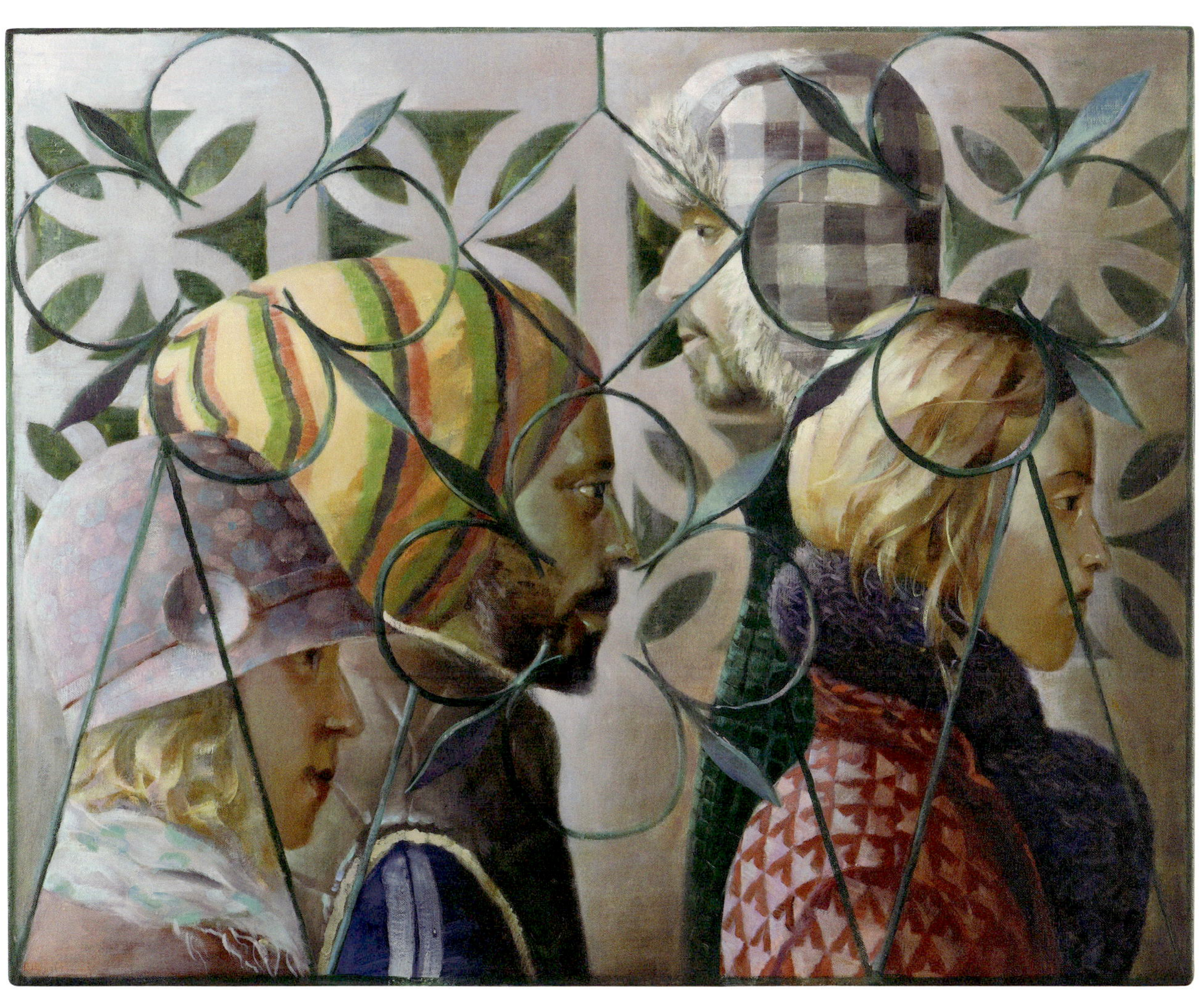

The Yellow Shop, 2014
Oil on linen, 51 × 76 cm
(detail overleaf)

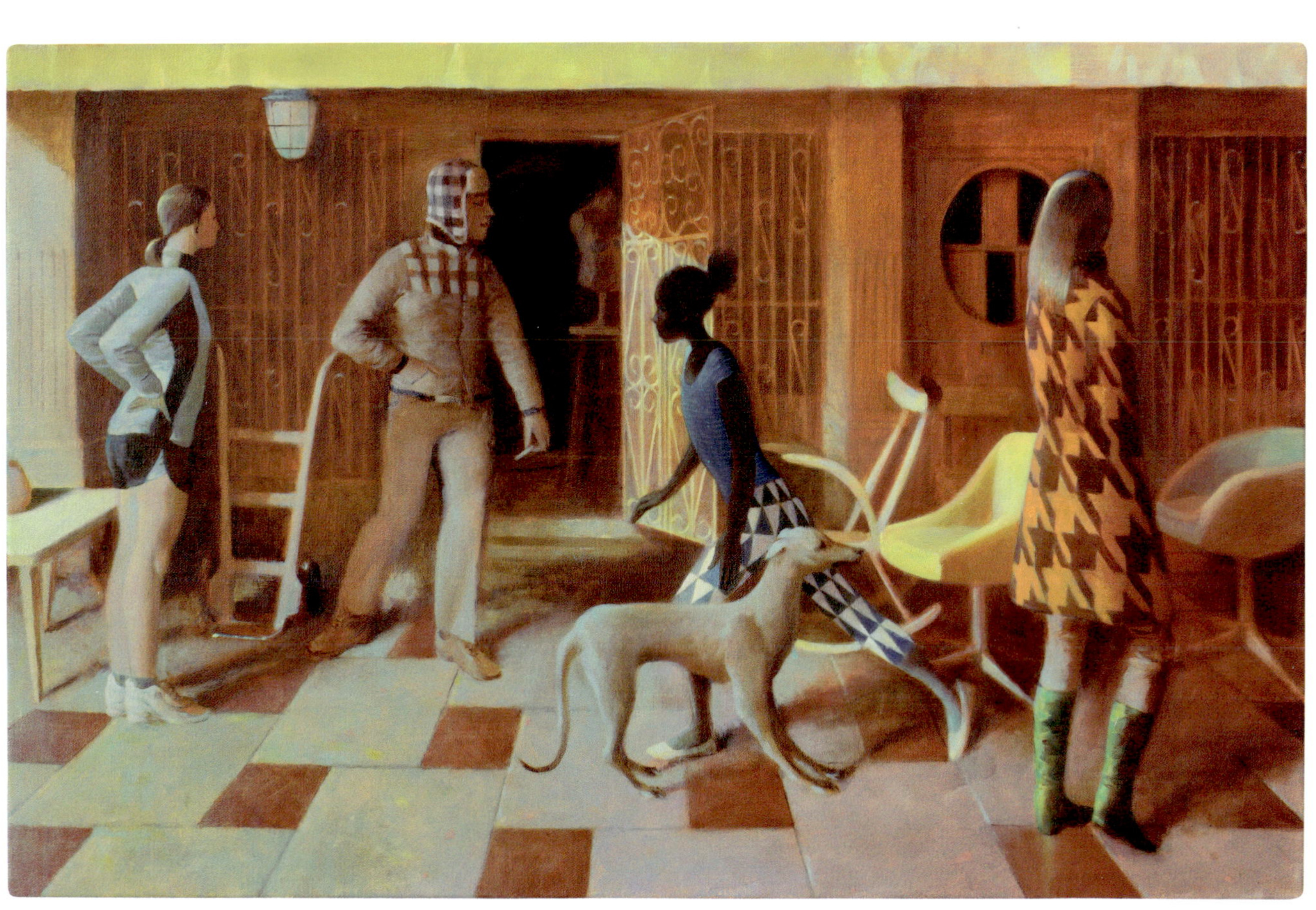

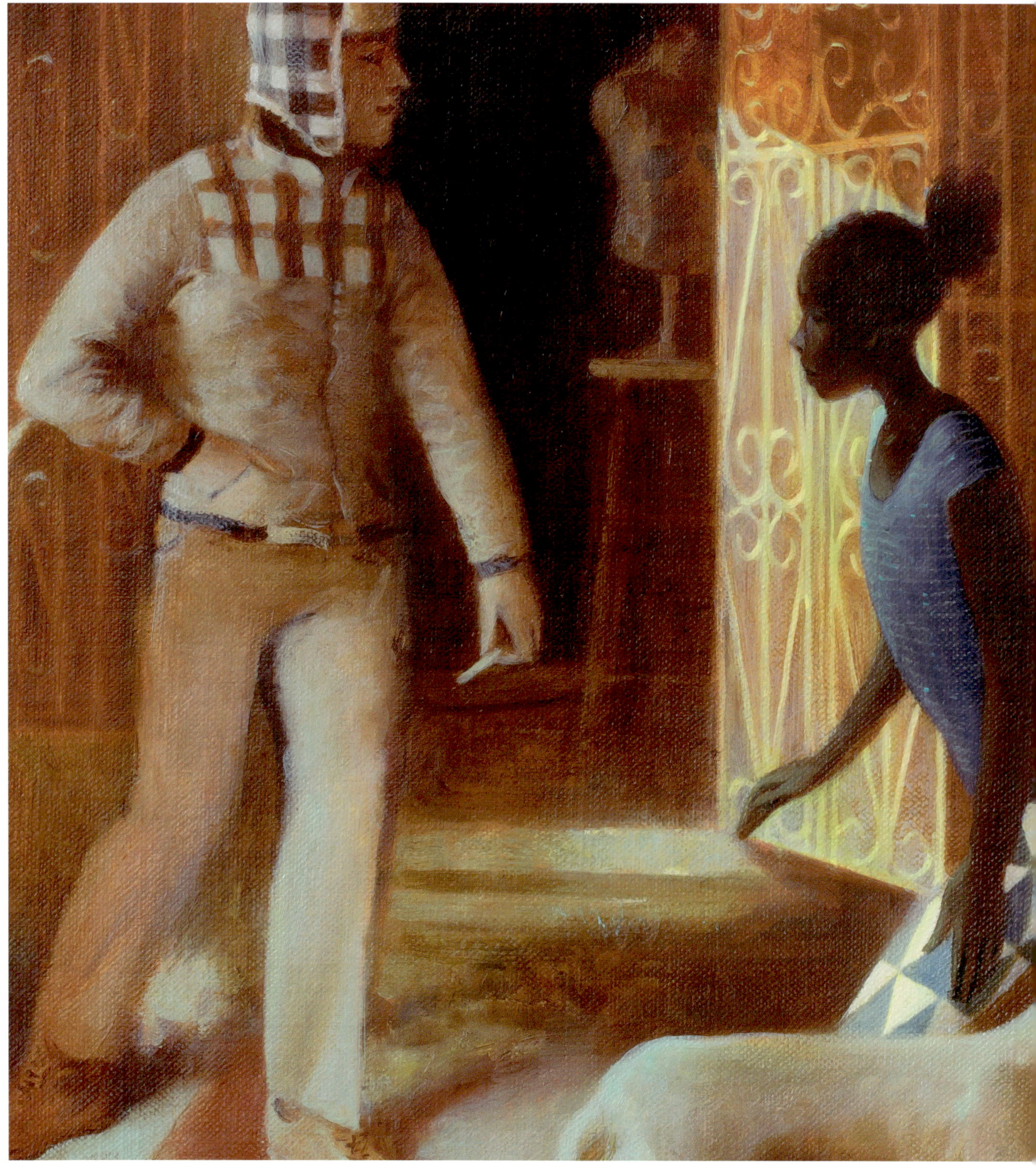

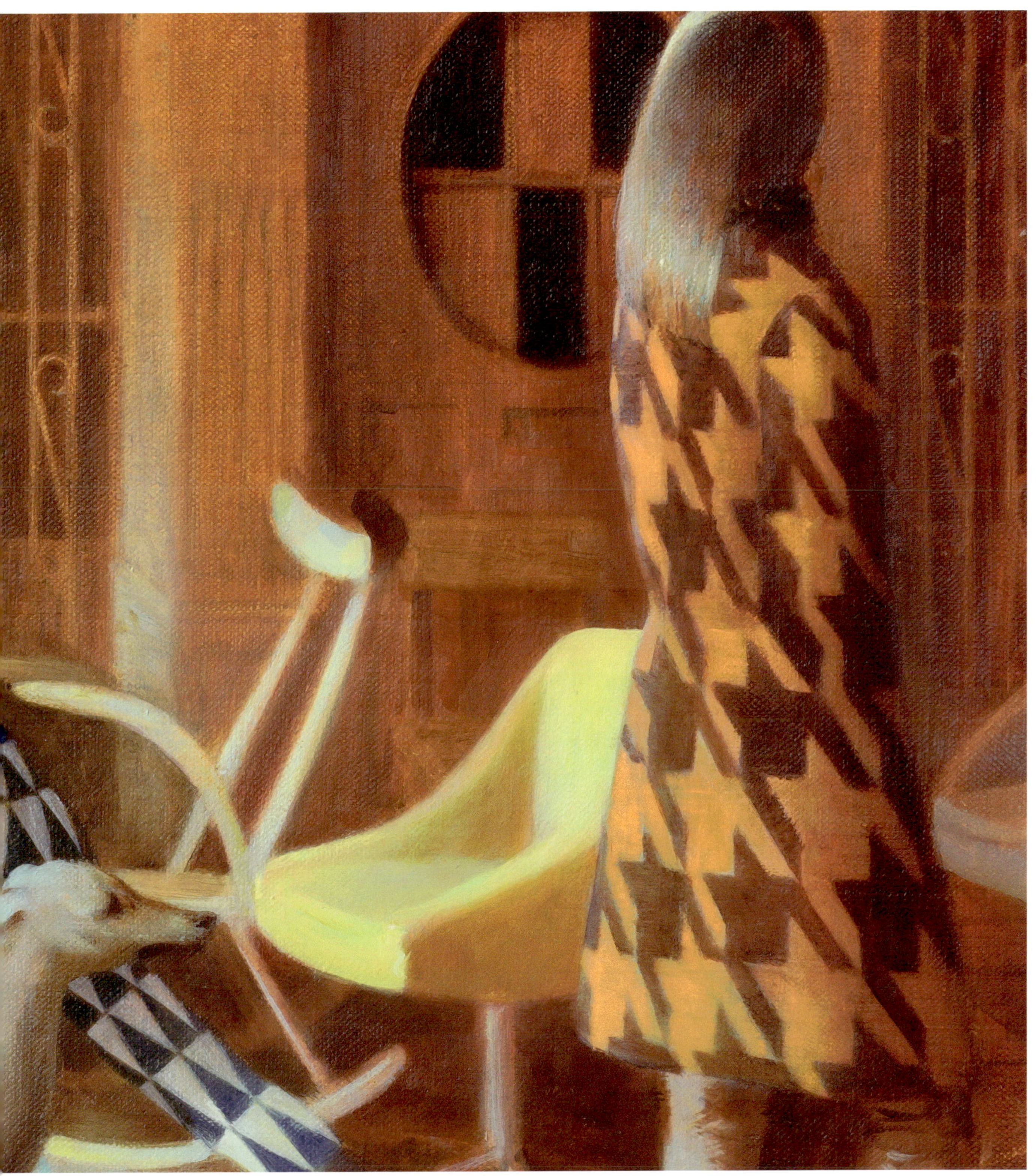

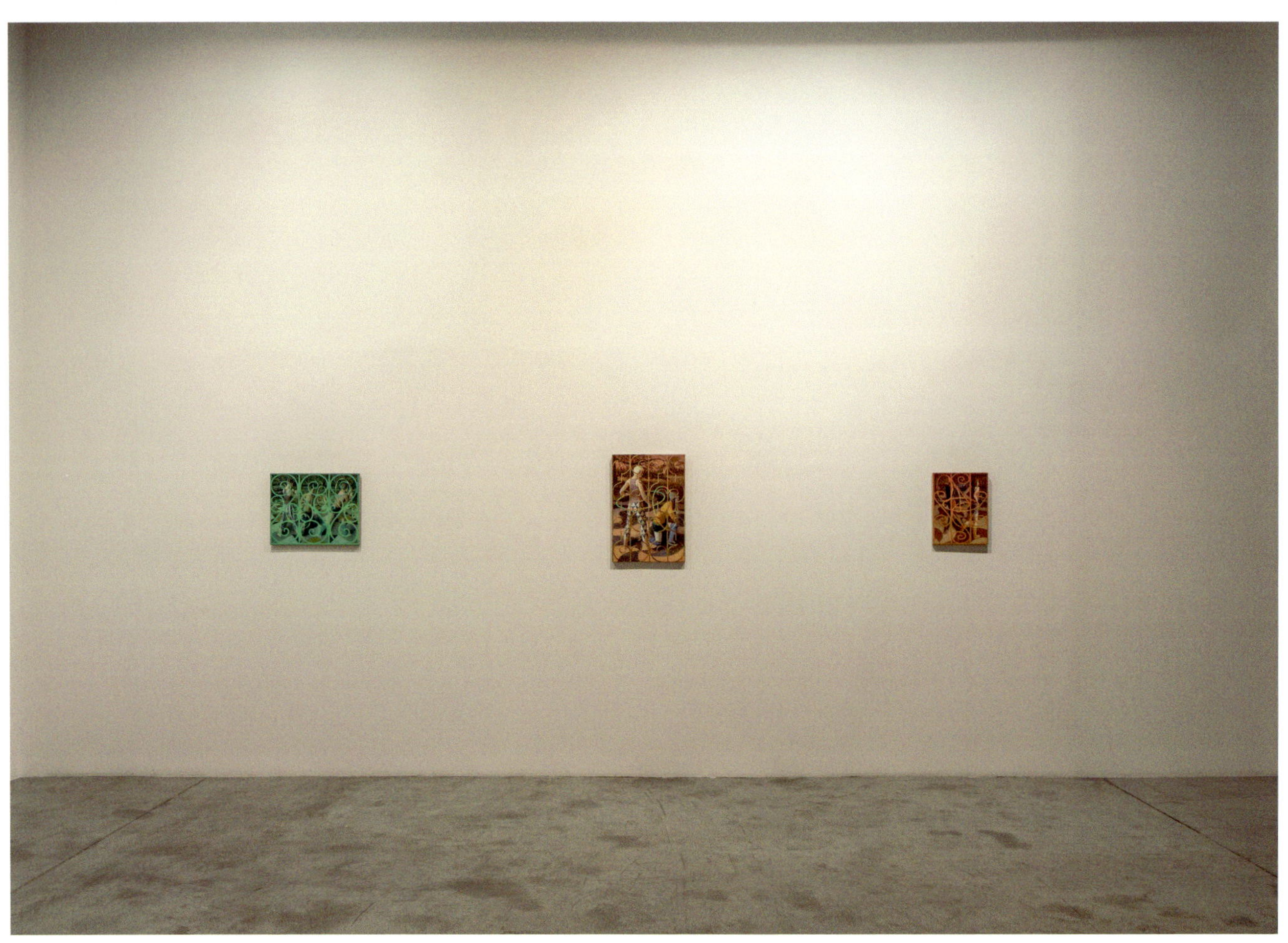

Installation views of the exhibition *Enclosure* at Grey Noise,
Dubai, 12 January – 21 February 2015

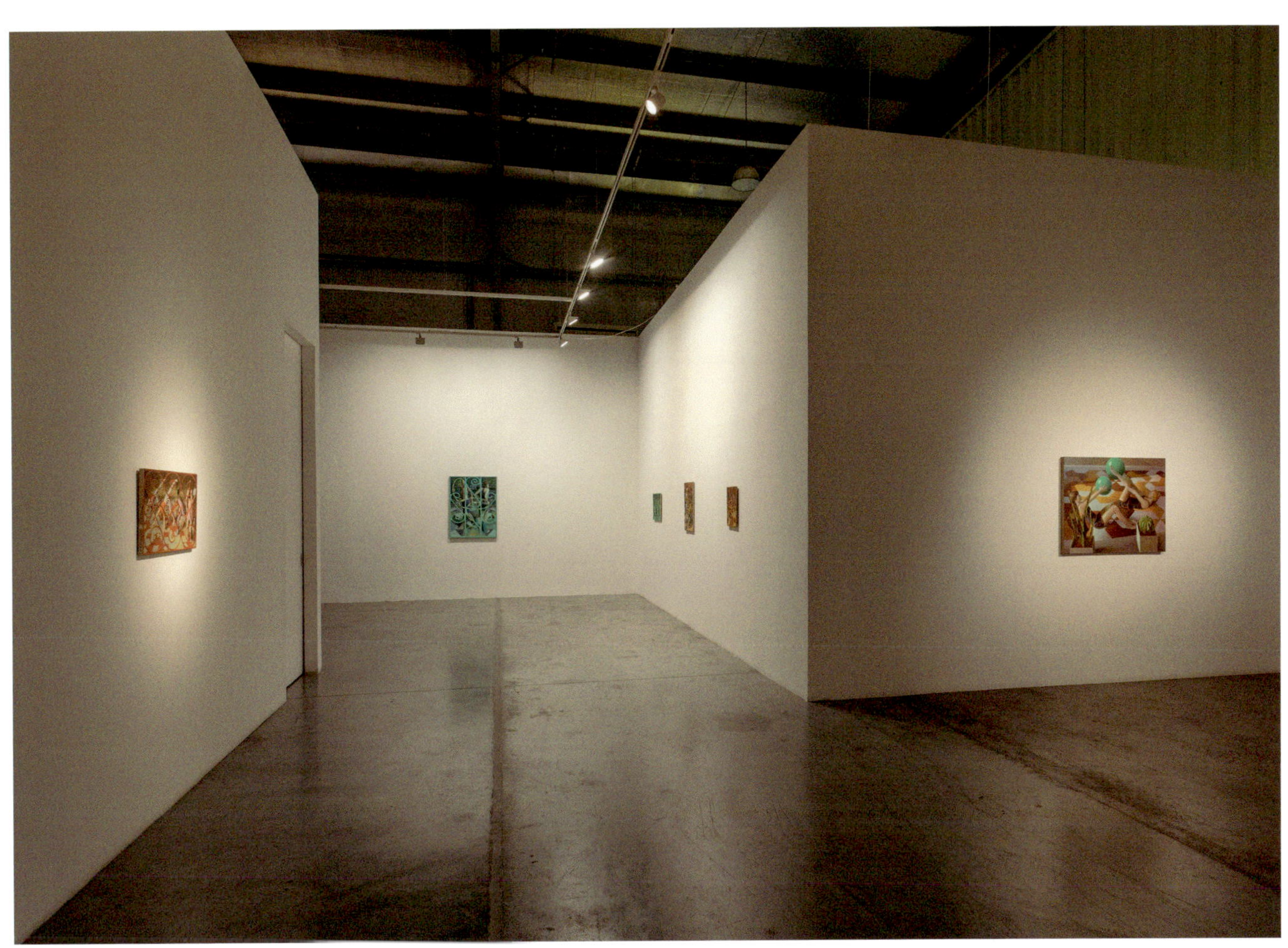

Colophon

Edited by Matt Price
Proofreading by William Lambie
Designed by Joe Gilmore / Qubik

Photography:
Musthafa Aboobacker: pp.98,
99; Anna Arca: pp.4, 75, 79; Andy
Keate: pp.7, 25, 36, 37, 55, 57, 59,
61, 63, 65, 67, 71, 80, 83, 87, 91,
93, cover; Jason Mandella: pp.18,
29, 33, 35, 39, 41, 43, 50, 51; Dave
Morgan: pp.27, 31, 45, 47, 49, 53,
69, 73, 77, 81, 82, 85, 89, 95, 96-7;
Benjamin Senior Studio: pp.8, 10,
12, 15, 17, 21, 23, 26

Cover image:
Detail of *Ball Games III*, 2013,
oil and egg tempera on linen,
70 × 100 cm (p.59)

First published in 2015 by
Anomie Publishing, England

www.anomie-publishing.com

ISBN: 978-1-910221-06-8

Printed by Pressision, England
Distributed by Casemate Art

Supported by:

BolteLang

MONICA DE CARDENAS GALLERIA

JAMES FUENTES